BROTHER ANDRÉ AS I KNEW HIM
Joseph Olivier Pichette's Testimony

A transcript of the original testimony
given by Joseph Olivier Pichette
for the cause of the beatification of Brother André

Lumière sur la Montagne   12

Research and Documentation Center
Saint Joseph's Oratory of Mount Royal
Montreal

September 2003

Translated from the original French by
Charles-Eric Doran

Revised by
Réto Davatz
and
Isabelle Bourbon

Copy Editing by
Allison Haggart

Editor
Daniel Picot

ISBN: 2-89483-012-2
Legal deposit – Third trimester 2003
National Library of Quebec
National Library of Canada

Printed in Canada

Cover art: Patrick Saad, *The Intention*, 2001
Cover graphic design: Michel Archambault
Inside photos graphic design: Ismaël Picot

About Joseph Olivier Pichette
(1886-1965)

In 1911 Joseph Olivier Pichette met Brother André for the first time. He was 25 years old and he became one of Brother André's great friends, intimates and allies for the next 27 years.

While employed in a shoe store he suddenly began suffering from severe pains and haemorrhages of the stomach and throat and from a weakened heart which let him almost dying. Through the intercession of saint Joseph, Brother André obtained his healing and he lived almost 80 years. Pichette's given name, Olivier, was then replaced with Joseph as a mark of gratitude for the great favours received. For this reason he was henceforth known as "Joseph Pichette". He directly witnessed at least 26 other cases of inexplicable cures through Brother André's prayer. Later with his wife he participed in the fulfilment of one of Brother André's fondest dreams when he offered the XIIth Station of the *Way of the Cross* in the Gardens of the Oratory, a *Calvary* carved out of Indiana natural buff stone (Photo p. 85).

In 1941, at the age of 54, he was the first out of 49 witnesses who testified at the "Information Trial" in Montreal for the cause of the beatification of Brother André, the « Miracle Man of Mount Royal » who had changed his whole life.

Almost a Family Life in The Oratory

During the August Novena of 1965, as perhaps Brother André's closest friend, Joseph Olivier Pichette, then 79 years old, accompanied by his son Dollard, met Father Marcel Lalonde, c.s.c. (Rector of St Joseph's Oratory from 1962 to 1992).

In 1911, Joseph Olivier Pichette met Brother André for the first time. The young man was then aged 25 and suffered from a heavy heart condition, haemorrhages of the throat and stomach. In 1941, he was the first witness who testified in the hearings for the cause of the beatification of Brother André.

Photos credit : Saint Joseph's Oratory of Mount Royal

THE TESTIMONY OF
JOSEPH OLIVIER PICHETTE
ON BROTHER ANDRÉ[*]

Given at the Diocesan Information Trial in Montreal[1]

[Identity of the Witness]

Pichette, Joseph Michel Olivier, French Canadian. My father's name was Olivier Pichette. My mother's name was Marie-Louise Gareau. I am 54 years old, married, bourgeois[2] and a former tradesman of average wealth.

[Origin of His Acquaintance with Brother André]

(Ad. 11[3]): I knew Brother André personally for almost thirty years. I would see Brother André at least a hundred to one hundred and fifty times a year. Quite often, about fifteen times each year for twenty-five years, we would sleep in the same room. After a long illness, he spent four weeks at my home and in June of 1936, he spent three weeks at my cottage in Rawdon[4].

---

[*] The original french text is the property of the Archdiocesis of Montreal, printed in Rome along with other documents under a latin title: *Fratris Andreae, Positio super virtutibus.* It has been first published in French by the Research and Documentation Center in *Cahiers de l'Oratoire Saint-Joseph* (number 4, June 1998) with the authorization of the cardinal Archbishop of Montreal. The following english translation has been made from that text.

[1] Since a reform in 1983, some expressions from the code of *Canon Law* have changed. For instance, today we would use the term 'inquiry' over that of 'trial'. However in this translation some archaisms have been deliberately kept in order to preserve some of the spirit of the original text.

[2] Mr. Pichette introduces himself as a « bourgeois », according to a usage not yet regarded as pejorative, but which simply indicated a social status.

[3] The mention *"Ad.* 11" means *"At question* 11" (the witness replies...). This is why we shall, from now on, use the mention "(Q. 12, etc.)" for *Question.*

[4] Mr. Pichette lived in a northern part of Montreal and owned a summer cottage in the small town of Rawdon in the area of Joliette.

He was very ill. I was very close to him. He would inquire about our business, our friends, and he would talk about the Oratory. On the whole, he treated me as a good friend.

(Question 12): Every day I heard a lot of people talk about Brother André. People knew that I frequently went to the Oratory, so it gave them a reason to do so as well. Generally, these people would tell me about favours and graces obtained at the Oratory.

(Q. 13): What I know about Brother André, I know through personal contact, through having seen Brother André and hearing others talk about him. I learned a few things from my reading of the life of Brother André by Reverend Father Bergeron, c.s.c. I do not wish to relate details from this book, but rather, I will speak exclusively of what I have learned first-hand.

(Q. 14): I have a great devotion to Brother André. Since he passed away, I entrust him with asking Saint Joseph for favours I wish to obtain. When he was alive, I often asked him to pray to Saint Joseph for me. I have great confidence in Brother André. He obtained so many favours for me and for others and I have seen so many others obtain favours from him. I often saw him pray when he was alive and seeing him so pious and fervent inspired me with confidence.

[The Childhood and Adolescence of Brother André]

(Q. 16): Brother André was born on August 9, 1845, in Saint-Grégoire d'Iberville.

(Q. 17): He told me that his mother was very good to him. He once told me about a time when he had been invited out for an evening. Having arrived a little early, he went for a walk before entering the house. As he was passing near a brook, a strange noise caught his attention. Remembering that the people who had invited him were not very good Catholics, he said to his mother, "Mother, if you don't want me to go to this place, let me hear that noise again," and the noise occurred once more. He did not go out that evening. He told me that his mother was very devout. He was the sixth child in a family of ten children. I observed that Brother André had not received much schooling as his parents were poor, yet according to what he had told me about his mother's piety, I believe the children received a good Christian education.

(Q. 18): Urgently baptised at home, for having almost died at birth, he was then taken to church the next day to fulfil the ceremony of Baptism. I know that he was christened Alfred.

(Q. 20): His father died five years after Brother André's birth and he was twelve years old when his mother died. He told me that from the age of twelve and onwards, he lived with an uncle.

(Q. 23, *trial,* p. 47)[5]: Brother André knew how to read. He must have learned a little in elementary school and improved his reading skills on his own, with practice. According to what Brother André told me, I can infer that he started working at a young age; that is, after his mother's death, at the age of twelve.

(Q. 26): He must have been around twenty years old when he left Canada for the United States. He went there in order to earn a living.

(Q. 27): He never told me how he fulfilled his religious duties during adolescence. He told me that despite his feebleness, he did not let anyone outmatch him at work.

---

[5] The term *'trial,* p.' refers to the original notes from the trial from which the *summarium* draws excerpts.

(Q. 28): He told me that his uncle was hard on him. He was robust and he expected others to be able to perform the same work he did. Having to bend over all day, working as a shoemaker, did not facilitate his digestion. It made me believe that Brother André had already accepted the hardships and miseries of work, despite his fragile health.

(Q. 32): He once mentioned something about the parish priest Father André Provençal from Saint-Césaire, telling me that he was a good pastor. I do not know much of his life previous to the time he entered the community.

[His Religious Life]

(Q. 34, *trial,* p. 51): In 1870, Brother André entered the Noviciate of the Congregation of Holy Cross in Saint-Laurent. He told me that afterwards, he was sent to Notre-Dame-des-Neiges College[6] in Montreal.

(Q. 36): He told me that he was frequently ill at the time of his noviciate, that he suffered from poor digestion.

Having once learned that His Excellency Bourget, Bishop of Montreal, was visiting the community, Brother André went to him and told him about his worries concerning his health and that he feared the community would not keep him because of his poor health. Bishop Bourget received him as a son, reassured him and told him that the community would keep him. Brother André added that from then on he had no more worries about the matter.

(Q. 37): He joined the community and became a brother in 1870, the very year that Pius IX proclaimed Saint Joseph Patron of the Universal Church. He entered at the age of twenty-five

---

[6] By 'college' we are referring to a private institution; in this case one where boys as young as 6 years old were schooled.

and must have been twenty-six at the time of his profession of faith.

I heard that Pastor Provençal, from the parish of Saint-Césaire, wrote a letter of recommendation to the priests of the Holy Cross in favour of the young Bessette. It said, among other things, "I am sending you a saint."

(Q. 38, *trial,* p. 52): I do not know what his occupations were at the time of his noviciate in Saint-Laurent. He once told me that at Notre-Dame College, he was appointed porter and that each week, he had to bring and pick up the children's clothes at the households. He had a carriage for that purpose. He was also responsible for waking the pupils and the religious of the community.

He helped the youngest children attend to their needs in the washroom.

He told me that he acted as college barber, cutting the children's hair. He provided all kinds of services for the children and even for his fellow religious and his work would extend into the night.

At night when he withdrew to his room, he would mend his cassock. He made his own pants and slippers. As for his undergarments, he never made any for the simple reason, he used to say, that [he] never wore any.

He worked on the sashes for the priests of the community. He told me that the tassel at the end of the sashes was difficult to make because he had been given a faulty model. He made one out of wood, covered it with cloth and it has subsequently been used as the model for all the sashes of the community.

He confessed to me that often, he hardly had time to jump into bed before it was already waking time.

He recounted to me that on one Sunday, a woman who had come to see her child went to Brother André. She told him she found that he had changed. Laughing, he replied, "I change every Sunday. There is nothing extraordinary about that."

For forty years, he had been a porter, so he would laughingly say, "When I became a brother, my superiors showed me the door and I stayed there for forty years."

He worked practically all day and all night. I am convinced that if I thought longer about it, I would find many other things to say.

[The Shrouding of the Dead]

He was frequently called upon to shroud dead people. A man from Côte-des-Neiges had died and Brother André had known him well. This man had told Brother André that should he die first, he would like to be shrouded by him. After this man's death, which occurred in the morning, his wife sent her child to ask Brother André to shroud him. Brother André told him that he was too busy then but that he would go in the evening. The woman sent her child back with the message that it would be too late. Brother André told the child to reassure his mother, that there would still be enough time in the evening.

He went there around five o'clock. The woman had covered the corpse with a large white sheet. He then proceeded to wash and dress the body. As he was putting on the socks, he noticed that the head of the corpse had changed position. He set it upright and then noticed that the corpse, which had not yet attained the stiffness common to the dead, had only now begun to stiffen. The brother noted, "I believe he waited for me to shroud him; for when I proceeded to wash him, it seemed as though he had just died."

Brother André indicated to me that, each time he returned to the college, after having shrouded a deceased person, something would occur which prevented him from sleeping.

He once told me that on the same evening in which he had shrouded the deceased man, under the circumstances I have just mentioned, he walked around the community house and went to bed around midnight. He began to hear noises and got up several times until he finally saw something like a black cat walking among the glasses in a cupboard, yet nothing was broken.

According to this event, I can gather that there was some extraordinary force which disturbed his sleep in order to discourage him from shrouding the deceased.

[Life in a Religious Community]

Quite often, he went with the children for walks through the streets of the city. The children liked to go with him and despite the fact that for many of them their homes were located near the college, he indicated that he never lost a child on the way.

His superior once expressed that he wished Brother André arrange the grounds in front of the college. The field was stony and the grass grew in patches. "I took the responsibility," he said, "to arrange the site. Using two wheelbarrows, I set about carting the stones and dead weed a great distance from the college. It was wearisome but I intended to succeed." He also confessed that he took time from his sleeping hours to do this work. Sometimes, when he had to catch up on his prayers, he would carry a barrow full of stones a great distance, and while he came back to get the another, he would say a part of his prayers. He added that sometimes he would work like this until morning and it did not tire him too much.

He also had to clean the windows of the college; a task he found very hard.

Once, as he was cleaning the windows, he started to spit blood. The physician who examined him advised him to stop working so hard, for it could exhaust him to death. The physician met the superior and warned him of the risk Brother André was taking of haemorrhaging. The superior discussed this with Brother André to which he replied, "Father Superior, would it matter to you if I didn't die in the house?" The superior told him it would not, so Brother André retorted, "Then if it doesn't matter to you, it doesn't matter to me whether I die in the house

11

or while cleaning the windows." So the superior let him resume his work.

Miss Marcotte, now Dr. Vidal's wife, related to me that she was a young girl when Brother André used to deliver her brother's clothes, who was then student at Notre-Dame des Neiges College. One winter's day, Brother André came as usual and chatted with the family with whom he was acquainted. At some point, Miss Marcotte's mother pointed out that it was cold in the house and wondered whether the furnace had gone out. Brother André bid them not to bother about it as he went down to attend it himself. Miss Marcotte added that this religious did not seem to fear hard work as he emptied the furnace and lit it up again.

Once in a while, his help was required in the kitchen. One day His Excellency Bruchési, Archbishop of Montreal, came unexpectedly to the college to have a meal. The brother cook called for Brother André to help him. He went there and began peeling potatoes. He was surprised to hear that Archbishop Bruchési was asking for him, insisting that he should sit at the table next to him. As he told me this story, he added, "I would rather have spent the whole day peeling potatoes."

He would also sweep the floors in the evening, at night or in the morning; whenever he could.

One day, having just swept and scrubbed floors all night, some nuns asked him whether he had found time to attend mass. He replied laughing, "Though I have spent the night scrubbing, I nonetheless received communion this morning." He was making a pun. Here in Canada, the expression 'to scrub' may also mean, to drink heavily[7].

(Q. 39, *trial,* p. 58): I was not acquainted with him in the first years of his religious life, but for the entire time I knew him,

---

[7] (Tr.'s n.) The exact term is the French verb 'brosser', which can either mean 'to brush' or 'to scrub'.

I observed that whatever he undertook, he would do to perfection.

Personally, I do not know whether he neglected the duties of his station to pray at the chapel while he was porter at the college. What I do know is that in all the years I knew him, he never neglected any of his religious duties.

(Q. 40): He would tell me that illness should not be used as an excuse for preventing one from fulfilling one's duties. He was the very opposite of a creature of comfort. He never wanted help. At the Oratory, he would often go to bed very late, but was up at four-thirty every morning. He would not choose his tasks. I think that what I have previously said proves this very well.

[His State of Health: An Impediment or a Means for Spiritual Growth?]

(Q. 41): It seems to me that his state of health was, a means of sanctification for him. When he was too ill to do any work, he spent that time in prayer.

During his time at my home when he was seriously ill, it was not uncommon to find him with a rosary in hand. Since he could not read, my wife offered to read for him which he gladly accepted.

[His Prayer and His Faithfulness to the Rules of the Community]

(Q. 42): When we happened to sleep in the same room at the Oratory, I know he would get up at four-thirty in the morning. He explained to me that he needed time to prepare everything so that he could be on time for communal meditation.

In the evening when he would leave his room from the community house to go to the room where he slept at the Oratory, he would frequently look into his meditation book and say, "Well, tomorrow I shall meditate on that topic."

13

Five minutes prior to the three o'clock Hour of Adoration, he could no longer keep still. He would then leave any visitor or anybody else in order to be on time for the service. I believe that he was later exempted by his superiors from that duty.

During the time I knew him, it seemed that he was exempted from quite a number of community exercises.

Before the presbytery was built, he slept above the small chapel.

Once the presbytery was built, his superiors allowed him to sleep in the small chapel as long as there was someone else there with him.

It is my understanding that he slept at Notre-Dame College during the first years of the Oratory. Once the chapel was built, he would spend his nights in the little room above the chapel, since, I believe, he did not want to leave it unguarded. It was located on the mountain, some distance from the college. He slept in this little chapel until the presbytery was built. I do not believe he ever slept in that room without his superiors' permission.

He looked after this chapel for which he was appointed sacristan. He told me that sometimes, after visiting sick people, he would sweep the floors late in the evening and even at night.

(Q. 43, *trial,* p. 64): During the time I knew him, Brother André prayed practically all day long. I would see him almost every afternoon and, as I mentioned at the last hearing, he never missed the Office of the Blessed Sacrament until he was exempted by his superiors. I had said at the last hearing that he would frequently tell me about his meditations. In the evening before he would get some rest in his small room above the former chapel of the Oratory, he would glance at his meditation book, saying, "Tomorrow I shall meditate on this."

I have also said that in the morning he would wake up earlier than the rest of the community because he wanted to be ready at the same time as the others for meditation.

I have also said that when he was ill and would come to rest at my home in Montreal, he complained that he had to catch up on his meditations because of his poor health. My wife offered to read him his meditations and he gladly accepted. All these little facts prove to me that he was faithful to his exercises of piety.

According to the community rules, he had to have a Holy Hour once a week, but would do many in a week.

He often invited someone to do the Hour of Adoration with him. The Hour of Adoration was held in the evening after his visits to the sick, and Brother André would recite or read prayers as his assistant held a candle. Little by little, the people who did the Hour of Adoration with him grew in number. This practice was the precursor to the Holy Hour held every Friday evening at Saint Joseph's Oratory.

To those who came to him, he would speak of obedience, making comparisons on the matter in order to show that the will of the superiors is the will of God. I deduce from this that merely by matter of obedience, he must have been faithful to his devotions.

In the last years of his life, since he would receive sick people practically all day long, often very early in the morning and sometimes late in the evening, I believe that his superiors exempted him from many community exercises.

I know that even in his last years, he was a devout early riser.

This may have been because he postponed his exercises until evening and would then pray in the chapel for such a long time at night.

I have spent entire days almost always by his side as I watched the door of the office where Brother André received the sick and the afflicted. I would see him on his way to receive communion at the six o'clock mass.

In the days of the small chapel, he fulfilled nearly all the functions as sacristan or serving mass for example. He told me that one morning he had served eight masses.

He received people all morning long and at five minutes to twelve, he would leave the presbytery.

After receiving communion, he would spend twenty to thirty minutes with his head down over the prie-dieu. He always attended two or three masses.

I know that he used to go to confession to Father Laurin, c.s.c., in Saint-Laurent. Often when we rode by car, he would ask me to make a stop in Saint-Laurent and I knew that the reason was so he could go to confession.

The first time he went to Saint-Laurent to confess to Father Laurin, c.s.c. was when he was ill and resting at my home in Montreal,

He would do the Way of the Cross every day, often accompanied by some of his lay friends. This Way of the Cross would last nearly an hour as Brother André knelt down on the path, his head bent, reciting special prayers as he was not bound by any formulation.

When we slept in the same room at the Oratory, he would ask me to pray with him at night. He would start saying the rosary and go on to say two more. He would do the same thing all over again before going to bed.

Right before bedtime, he would still be praying and ask me to pray with him. Some nights he was so tired that he asked me to let him sleep for fifteen minutes, and when he woke up, he would pray again. Sometimes he went down to the chapel under the room and prayed there for much of the night. One night I was worried, so I went down. He was kneeling, his head was bent forward and he was praying.

When I drove him late at night, he would pray the whole way back to Montreal.

When he was alone in his office, which happened sometimes in the fall or in the winter, I never went in without seeing him reading a book of piety, of meditation, or of the life of a saint.

To my knowledge, he observed all of God's commandments and of the Church. Judging from the conversations he had with us, I am sure he observed them all.

[His Devotions]

(Q. 44, *trial,* p. 68): To those who visited him, he seemed to recommend having a devotion to something they did not yet have a devotion to. To someone who had a strong devotion to Saint Joseph, he would advise devotion to the Blessed Virgin or to the Passion of Our Lord.

He had a great devotion to the Passion of Our Lord and would often speak about it with tears in his eyes. When he wanted to convert a sinner, he would take from his desk a statue of Our Lord covered with blood. With love, he would speak about Our Lord who had suffered and died for them.

His most important devotion was to the Passion of Our Lord. He taught that devotion to the Blessed Virgin should never be separated from devotion to Saint Joseph, to Our Lord or to the Holy Family.

He also had a devotion to the Blessed Virgin and of course, to Saint Joseph. He often recommended that we pray to the Sacred Heart and to the Precious Blood of Jesus.

He had read much on the works of Saint Gertrude and knew many prayers that she had written.

He also had a great devotion to Our Lady of the Seven Sorrows. He often said the Rosary of the Seven Wounds.

[His Devotion to the Passion of Our Lord]

(Q. 45): When he visited the sick, he would speak about Saint Joseph and would pray to him.

He cherished the devotion to the Passion of Our Lord. Once, at my summer cottage, a man whose behaviour left much to be desired requested to see Brother André, who welcomed him and

17

spoke to him in such a way about Our Lord suffering and dying for him, that the man was deeply moved, and I believe that he mended his ways. Brother André spoke to him about the Passion for more than three hours. We were listening, my wife and I, and we were both moved. His face was tensed. Brother André's visitor thanked him with tears in his eyes. As I drove him home, the man said to me, "Mr. Pichette, a thousand dollars couldn't have kept me away from this evening."

All of his devotions seem to have founded upon that of the Passion of Our Lord.

I often heard Brother André recommend other devotions than that of a devotion to Saint Joseph.

He attempted by all means possible to spread the devotion to the Passion. Should he have wished to convert a sinner, he would shut himself in his office and spend an hour with said sinner. No matter how insistently other visitors knocked at the door, he would not answer. He would then speak about the Passion of Our Lord and would not quit until he had won the sinner over.

He would then take a statuette from his desk, an *Ecce Homo* statuette of Our Lord, and would describe His Scourging and Crowning. He told me on two or three occasions that Our Lord had been struck 6666 times. He probably considered that each knot from each lash produced a stroke.

We owe to Brother André the devotion to the Way of the Cross as it exists today at the Oratory.

One evening he was having dinner at my home and I remember his joy as he announced to me that there would be a Way of the Cross enacted at the Oratory. It was in the spring prior to his death. I had never seen Brother André so happy. He was thrilled since the Way of the Cross gave way to many conversions.

He often recommended the devotion to the Way of the Cross, not only to his close friends, but also to his visitors.

[His Devotion to Saint Joseph]

When people came to Brother André to tell him about misfortunes, he would always answer, "Pray to Saint Joseph. Do novenas to Saint Joseph." He often talked to me about Saint Joseph's life, sufferings and tribulations.

He would recommend to the afflicted people to pray to Saint Joseph and to say to him, "If you were in my place, Saint Joseph, what would you want to happen? Well then, let it be done to me!"

He advised the sick to rub the afflicted limb with Saint Joseph's oil and with a medal of Saint Joseph, until the pain would cease. Saint Joseph's oil consisted of olive oil that burned in front of the statue of Saint Joseph.

He advised the sick to rub themselves often and for long periods of time; for he wished the rubbings would last at least an hour.

He told someone to rub himself for a long time because it was both an act of love and of faith.

To some, he would advise prayers and novenas to Saint Joseph, while to others, to rub themselves frequently.

A certain person, I believe he was a bishop, once said to Brother André, "It's strange, Brother André, you tell some people that they are cured and it's done. Others you advise to pray to Saint Joseph, to do novenas. Others you advise to rub themselves with a medal or to use Saint Joseph's oil yet to others you tell that you shall pray for them. What is the difference?" to which Brother André replied, "Sometimes it's quite easy to see."

When he rubbed someone, he would use his hand rather than a medal and said it produced the same results.

To those who told him about family problems or about lawsuits made against them, he would recommend that they hold a medal of Saint Joseph in their hand.

19

To those who feared the outcome of a lawsuit, he advised sending a medal to the lawyer working for the other side or to the judge.

He once advised a travelling salesman to hold a medal of Saint Joseph in his hand when meeting a customer. The man later told Brother André that it had worked wonders. He admitted frankly that he had been unsuccessful on only one occasion. He was referring to the occasion when he had tried to make me one of his clients as I had been holding a medal so that this salesman would not succeed!

When he advised someone to rub himself, he also advised that he pray to Saint Joseph.

Since the beginning of his apostolate, as early as when he was porter at Notre-Dame College, he advised people to rub themselves with a medal.

Before the apostolate of Brother André began, devotion to Saint Joseph was not as widespread [as it is today]. It is to Brother André that we owe the spread of this devotion in Montreal and everywhere else. With Brother André, the Saint Joseph's Oratory was born.

At the masses held at the Oratory, about eighty to ninety percent of those in attendance are young people. Such devotion was inspired by Brother André.

I owe my great devotion and confidence in Saint Joseph to Brother André.

Brother André found it strange that out of so many people taking vacations, so few spent them at the Oratory.

He devoted his life to promoting Saint Joseph and quite successfully so, for the numerous pilgrimages to the Oratory attest to this.

When he visited sick people, he recommended that they pray to Saint Joseph and have faith in him. To those who were gravely ill, he recommended that they place themselves in the hands of Saint Joseph, the patron saint of the dying.

[The Beginnings of the Oratory]

(Q. 46, *trial,* p. 75): A priest once told Brother André, "It's curious. Each time I enter my room, I find the statue of Saint Joseph facing the mountain," and Brother André replied, "That means he wants to be honoured on the mountain."

At Notre-Dame College, he cured a child at the infirmary. The child told him that he was sick. Brother André rubbed him and the child, whose temperature had gone down, went back to class.

When the physician arrived, he was not pleased to learn that the child was back in class.

One day, Brother André had to deliver a message and asked a brother to replace him. This brother also had to go out, and so the superior of the community had to work as the porter at the parlour. When Brother André returned, the superior chastised him for his absence and made him kiss the ground as punishment. Brother André sought no excuse and executed the punishment.

Brother André recommended that the pupils' parents to pray to Saint Joseph. Little by little, the visitors to the college grew in number. They were either sick themselves or bringing sick people with them.

Seeing this crowd of sick people coming to the college, the pupils' parents complained to the superior threatening to remove their children for fear of contamination. Consequently, the superior forbade Brother André from receiving sick people. Brother André submitted to his superior's order.

People came anyway, but remained outside the college. Facing such insistence, the superior allowed Brother André to receive these people in a little station built by the Tramway Company. This system must have lasted for a few years.

He collected two hundred dollars by cutting children's hair and collecting alms he received from people he had cured. His superior allowed him to put that money aside.

In the early years after Brother André was appointed porter at Notre-Dame College, a man came to see him. Brother André inquired as to how things were going at home. The man answered, "What do you care?" Brother André told him that he did care. As the visitor realized that he had been somewhat rude, he explained his situation saying that his wife was ill and that he had many worries. Brother André told him, "I should think your wife isn't ill anymore. In fact, she is on her feet and will answer the door when you arrive." The man said, "Another prophet!" Everything happened as Brother André had said; the woman had been cured.

This event, along with the child's healing in the infirmary, must have contributed to Brother André's popularity and to the fact that sick people came to see him.

I have heard that Brother André was the scapegoat of the community at Notre-Dame College. When the Father Superior, a swift man, had something to say, he would take out his anger on Brother André who replied nothing and bore everything.

Brother André told me that he and Father Superior went to see His Excellency Bruchési, Archbishop of Montreal. His Excellency allowed them to build a chapel on the side of the mountain.

Father Superior and His Excellency allowed him to use the aforementioned two hundred dollars to build the chapel.

In the beginning, he erected a statue of Saint Joseph in a small niche on the side of the mountain, at the foot of which he placed a casket in which the people could deposit their alms.

Many offered him, among other things, free labour or donations in kind.

(*Trial*, p. 81): Even at the Oratory, while Reverend Father Dion was Superior, Brother André suffered because he felt uneasy with him and because the Reverend Father was rather harsh.

One day, a friend offered Brother André a ride to Sainte-Anne-de-Beaupré. Brother André replied, "I should ask my superior." His friend said to him, "Ask him, I will take care of all the expenses." The brother asked Father Dion for his permission and but was flatly turned down. Brother André submitted to the order and told his friend, "It does not suit my superior's wishes." His friend asked him, "If I obtain his permission, will you come?" Brother André answered, "Yes." And Brother André's friend obtained permission and so the pilgrimage to Sainte-Anne-de-Beaupré took place.

[Difficulties at the Beginning]

Brother André recounted to me that in the beginning, the Father Superior was not in favour of building the Oratory.

I have always been told that, in the beginning, his fellow religious were opposed to his cause. He told me that he encountered great difficulties at first, but mostly from outsiders.

These difficulties started while he was porter at the college, as I have said at the last hearing.

Complaints were made to Archbishop Bruchési by a delegation of the physician and a few notables from Côte-des-Neiges. They accused Brother André of being a charlatan and a feeler. His Excellency Bruchési received them but, nonetheless, allowed Brother André pursue his work.

Then the delegation complained to the Bureau of Health at the town hall.

A physician was sent to investigate. The physician went on the premises, made his inquiry and asked Brother André if he treated people and how. The brother gave him a medal of Saint Joseph and a bottle of Saint Joseph's oil telling him, "This is what I give people. You may use it yourself. You may find it useful." So the physician told him, "If you proceed this way, you have nothing to worry about; at least as far as the town hall is concerned. I see nothing wrong with what you're giving people."

Brother André told me that in those days he had a friend in whom he confided and with whom he would share his dreams and his disappointments. However, he realized that the man was betraying him, reporting all that was said while distorting facts.

[Mr. Malenfant]

When Brother André was about to build the chapel, a farmer from Rivière-du-Loup, a town situated three hundred miles from Montreal, had a dream. He felt that he was needed in Montreal to help a little man build a chapel. The very next day, he left his farm to one of his brothers and, despite the objections of his friends and family, he came to Montreal. He inquired about the one who wanted to build a chapel and was told that there was a poor brother in Côte-des-Neiges who wanted to build one. He went to Côte-des-Neiges and took the path leading to the small existing chapel that Brother André wanted to expand. They both met and Brother André told the man, "You are just the man I need," and he introduced him to his superior, Father Dion. Father Dion listened to the man (his name was Mr. Malenfant) but did not give the impression that he believed what the man said about his dream. As Mr. Malenfant left Father Dion's office, he felt discouraged and wanted to return home. Brother André told him to wait for a while. Two or three days later, Father Dion asked Brother André if the man had gone, as he wanted to meet with him. Mr. Malenfant came back and Father Dion accepted the proposal to work for the cause. For ten years he went all over the countryside, begging for alms and offering subscriptions to the magazine *l'Oratoire*.

I have recounted these facts as they are described by Father Bergeron in his *Life of Brother André*.

Father Clément, who was at the Oratory and now deceased, was also aware of these facts.

[The Construction of the Oratory]

The first small chapel on the mountain was built, I believe, in 1904. I was told that around 1890, Brother André had begun receiving and healing people at the parlour of Notre-Dame College.

This small chapel was later extended. In 1911, when I first visited the Oratory, it was large enough to accommodate eight to nine hundred people. The crypt that replaced the chapel was completed by mid-December 1916.

The construction of the basilica began around that time. The bare rock of the mountain had to be mined. Construction went on for many years.

Now the basilica is almost completed.

During the construction, a rich man (a millionaire) visited the site and admired all that was being done at the Oratory with so little money. I remarked to Brother André that it would require the visit of many millionaires to help him build the basilica. Brother André replied that Saint Joseph never had millions and that he was used to earning his living by the sweat of his brow.

People came to see Brother André and gave him donations, either asking that he pray for them or thanking him for a favour they had received.

From what I have seen myself, it is the accumulation of modest sums of money given by ordinary people that has made the construction of the Oratory possible.

In the evening, Brother André would put the money he had received during the day into a large black bag without counting it. When he decided there was enough money in the bag, he would ask to be excused in order to bring everything to his superior.

He used to say, "We must be strong through the hardships. We must endure everything for love of God. He suffered so much for us." I saw him one day at the door of the Oratory,

25

sobbing. He was with a man. I did not ask him why he was crying.

I have never personally seen him discouraged or demoralized.

[Brother André's Humility]

(Q. 47, *trial*, p. 87): As for the construction of the Oratory, he put everything in the hands of Saint Joseph, saying that God and Saint Joseph were very good.

I have been a witness to a miracle performed by Brother André. He told a sick person who had been brought to him on a stretcher, "Walk! Walk!" then went to the presbytery without any further preoccupation about the matter. The sick person walked! He was cured. There was great excitement in the crowd but Brother André had already left. He was probably having his lunch.

Brother André attributed the construction of the Oratory to Saint Joseph.

One day, a man came to Brother André and said to him, "When I pray to Saint Joseph I obtain nothing. When I ask you for favours, I obtain them." Brother André shuddered and had the man expelled.

To those who thanked him for having been healed, he invariably answered, "I didn't cure you. Saint Joseph did."

Since the holidays brought a great crowd to the Oratory, Brother André held himself aloof; he wanted to hide. He would not participate in processions unless he had to follow along with the community.

The chaplain to the King of England came to see Brother André and told him that the King wanted to meet with him. Brother André spoke with the chaplain for two or three minutes then said, "I beg your pardon, but there are many sick people."

It seemed to me that he gave preferential treatment to the poor over the rich.

I never heard Brother André boast by saying, "I have done this." He used to say that God uses instruments to do his work.

When he spoke about the construction of the Oratory, he would say, "Saint Joseph is very good. With such small sums we succeeded in doing all these things."

It would be difficult, in my opinion, to be humbler than Brother André.

[Encouragements Received]

(Q. 48, *trial,* p. 88): Besides His Excellency Archbishop Bruchési whom I have mentioned above, and Mr. Malenfant, Brother André was assisted by another layman, Mr. Maucotel.

As soon as His Excellency Archbishop Bruchési allowed the building of the Oratory, Reverend Father Dion, the superior of the community, and Reverend Father Clément, c.s.c. gave Brother André much encouragement. When Father Clément came to the Oratory, he was nearly blind. He could not read his breviary and could only say the mass of the Blessed Virgin or the Mass for the Dead. The physicians gave him no hope of getting better. He asked Brother André to restore his sight. Brother André said to him, "Tomorrow Father, you will be able to say your breviary and your mass." And so it happened. For many years, Father Clément could read his breviary and say his mass without wearing any glasses. He only wore glasses near the end of his life. The physicians who treated Father Clément's sight said they did not understand how this was possible.

Father Clément was the great auxiliary to Brother André at the Oratory and later on, so was Reverend Father Cousineau, c.s.c., now Superior General of the community.

In short, during the time I knew him, all his superiors helped and encouraged him.

His Excellency Archbishop Bruchési was quite in favour of the Oratory; a fact proven by the addresses he gave there.

[His Charity Towards His Fellowman]

(Q. 49): He recounted to me many facts from which one can clearly discern that he gave a lot of good advice to those who came to see him such as receiving the sacraments and prayers.

He loved the poor and welcomed them with even more sympathy than he did wealthier people. He always found a way of slipping in a good piece of advice, asking people to pray to God so that He may give them courage.

I do not think there were many visitors to whom he would not speak about Our Good Lord, the Passion of Our Lord or of Saint Joseph while always recommending that they pray, to see to it that others pray and that they do the Stations of the Cross.

He brought people to a better understanding of the love they owed God, making comparisons with the love they had for their wives, their children and their friends.

Among the works of corporeal mercy, I had said before, he shrouded the dead.

I have never brought a sick person to see Brother André who did not return satisfied. Some were cured, others died shortly after, but Brother André had comforted them all.

He would act this way with all the sick who came to see him.

Brother André often cried with those unfortunate people who told him of their miseries.

He made numerous visits to the sick.

When he would leave his office by five-thirty, he often visited the sick until late in the evening. Except in the last years and other than on Fridays, he spent every evening visiting sick people. I often went with him and he was always very nice to them.

I have been told that he also visited inmates.

[The Healings]

(Q. 50, *trial,* p. 94): The first time I heard about Brother André was from Mrs. Lucas who had come to my store knowing that I was ill. She told me that she once had a canker on an arm and went to see Brother André who told her to rub her arm with a medal of Saint Joseph, to put some Saint Joseph's oil on it and to drink some, if only a few drops. She told me that she had been cured and strongly recommended that I see Brother André myself. This was around 1911 or 1912.

A certain Mr. Bertrand, father of a travelling salesman in the shoe business, once had a canker on an arm that spread from wrist to elbow. (I had seen the photograph with my own eyes.) He had been miraculously healed by Brother André. It is Mr. Bertrand, the travelling salesman, who recounted this fact to me. Mr. Bertrand told me that Brother André had rubbed his brother[8] with a medal of Saint Joseph and had recommended that he do so as well, and his arm healed completely.

This was the second time I had heard about Brother André, and it must have occurred shortly after the healing of Mrs. Lucas.

[The Account of Mr. Pichette's Own Healing]

I then decided to see Brother André. I had previously asked my wife to see Brother André and tell him about my illness. Brother André asked her if I could come myself to which my wife replied, "Yes, on Sunday." Brother André then asked for me to come. He recommended that [my][9] wife get a medal of Saint Joseph and some Saint Joseph's oil, advising me to drink some even if I found it hard to digest. I went the following Sunday. Brother André asked me what I wanted. He told me to

---

[8] There is an ambiguity in the text, as to whether Mr. Bertrand was speaking of his brother or his father.

[9] (Translator's note): *Sic* "He had recommended his wife…"

wait, so I waited until all the other sick people had had their turn. When my turn came, he asked me to enter his office and to tell him my story, then asked me to come back every week, if possible. I saw him about a hundred times in the year following my first visit. I was not getting any better. I was being treated by Dr. Georges Aubry for throat and stomach troubles and I was spitting blood. The doctor told my sisters that my most serious problem was my heart condition and that he had never seen such a serious case of heart condition, whether in the hospitals of Paris or anywhere else that he had stayed. I could not digest anything and my kidneys and bowels were hardly functioning.

Dr. Aubry brought me to understand that by the end of the year I would have to get ready for the final journey, for nothing else could be done and no physician could do any better. I said there was still someone I could see and that I would not leave him unless I were either in my grave or on my feet again. I told him that it was Brother André. The physician said to me, "What are you thinking of, what can he do? He is an uneducated man. I have heard about him. They call him the 'old fool'." I replied that I trusted this man and that he [Brother André] could do at least as much as he. The physician added, "I warn you. Be very careful because on your way up to the Oratory, you could die at any moment."

The following Sunday afternoon I went up to the Oratory, met Brother André and told him what the physician had said to me. I said to Brother André, "If you allow me, I will stay here and will only leave if I am cured or in my grave. I can't live this way any longer. I am thinking of going off of my medication and bringing nothing of it here." The brother replied, "As you wish. If you want to come, you can sleep in my room in the small chapel." This is what I did. Brother André warned me not to walk too much, for I hardly ate anything and could risk a fatal injury. I still could not digest anything.

Nothing changed during the nine days I stayed at the Oratory. Brother André would rub me with his hand two or three times a day. On the ninth day, I believe he had rubbed me from eleven-thirty in the evening until two-thirty in the morning because whenever he asked me how I felt, I told him I was not feeling any better.

At that time, there were three of us who slept in his room. It was separated in two and he [Brother André] slept in the other part. I saw him get a small mattress out of his wardrobe, spread it out on the floor and lie on it without a pillow.

It was about a quarter past four in the morning when he was woken by his alarm clock. He got up and so did we. That night he brought out a piece of fresh pork, a piece of veal, some spices and seasoning, and put everything to simmer on the stove.

(*Trial,* p. 98): He peeled potatoes and he told me to add them to the broth the next morning by ten or ten-thirty.

At noon, he came for lunch. He took a large plate and filled it with meat, pasta and broth then offered me the plate. I objected, but he told me to eat and that everything would be fine. [I said,] "If you tell me so Brother André, I will eat." And he added three large pieces of bread.

When we had finished eating, Brother André said I could walk. I felt very well and spent the afternoon free of any pain. In the evening, Brother André inquired as to how I had been and I told him, "Everything went marvellously." In the evening, he served me the same food, about half the amount he had given me at noon. I went to bed at around ten-thirty that evening and slept until the next morning when Brother André's alarm clock woke me up. Up to that point, I had not slept a full night during the entire novena that I had spent at the Oratory.

The next day Brother André told me, "Since you are doing well, you may leave." I went home by tramway as I lived on the other side of the city. I took my bicycle and rode to Moreau train station, a few miles away from my residence. I took the train to Saint-Esprit, a village in the diocese of Joliette. I had to get off the train five miles from where I was going and since there was not a car in sight, I took my bicycle and rode to where I had to go.

It was a very hot August day when my cousin saw me arrive. He was with his family and my wife. My wife cried and I consoled her, telling her that I was cured. I was offered some pea-soup. I ate some and I had no feeling of discomfort. In the course of the three following weeks minus three days, I gained eighteen pounds.

These last three days, I spent back at the Oratory thanking the Lord for this cure.

The two friends I had left at the Oratory said to me, "Pichette, had we met you on the street, we would never have recognized you seeing as your health has improved so much."

Brother André told me, "The physicians are so much against me that you would be better off not going to see yours." So I did not go.

The same physician was treating my wife. I do not remember if it was on the occasion of my healing or of hers that Dr. Aubry said, "I have heard it before, so much the worse. It will all be over in a month."

I was cured thirty years ago. I have worked in my store for twenty-five years since it happened and though I was not entirely cured, I could still work without too much pain.

[Another Healing of Mr. Pichette by Brother André]

Brother André cured me on one other occasion. I had a canker on my right thumb. It happened seven or eight years later. It was August. I was at work when suddenly I noticed that I had a bruise and that blood was spurting out. I put something on the wound to stop the bleeding and for two weeks, the blood spurted out whenever I would squeeze something. I explained this to Dr. Rouleau, a friend of ours. He examined my thumb, saying it was a canker. He told me to go to Notre-Dame Hospital and see Dr. Panneton, who was in charge of X-ray treatments. I saw Dr. Panneton who, after examination and inquiring as to my age, also told me I had a canker. He offered to treat me with [ultra-] violet rays. During the course of the treatment, I felt that I was getting weaker. After the treatment, Dr. Rouleau advised me not to leave immediately, to lie down for a while, and that he would give me a ride back home. It was when I had the treatment when I began to suffer. The pain was increasing and my thumb was swelling. I went to see Brother André who rubbed me with a medal and told me to do so as well. I did not feel any better; instead, the pain was increasing.

On December the eighth, I had already not slept for some nights because I was suffering so much. I went to see Brother André in the afternoon. I told him I had never felt so bad. He replied, "In certain circumstances, sometimes it means that things are about to get better." He made me put a white cloth on the wound, rubbed it for five or six minutes, and whenever I had the misfortune of touching my thumb I felt a burning sensation. Brother André pressed very hard. After five or six minutes, Brother André told me that it would be enough. He removed the cloth. My thumb was normal and there only remained something like a black spot which I pointed out to Brother André and he said, "It's nothing." He scratched it with his nail. The black spot disappeared and two or three drops of blood came out. Brother André put the cloth back, rubbed my thumb again and everything was healed.

A woman had told me to put a piece of potato on my thumb. It took the pain away for a moment because it was cold. Brother André told me, "The potatoes you put on your thumb took the pain away. The doctors who treated you took your dollars away. As for Saint Joseph, he took everything away."

Later, I met with Dr. Rouleau. I had told Brother André that I would recount everything to my doctor. Brother André talked me out of it for the same reasons as with Dr. Aubry.

Dr. Rouleau asked me how my thumb was. I showed it to him, [and he said], "How strange, isn't it, that a single treatment could cure you? You should undergo some more treatments." I asked him, "You think that your treatment is the cause?" However, I did not go back to Dr. Panneton.

A few weeks later, the nurse who was working under Dr. Panneton's orders while I was undergoing treatments, came to my store to buy shoes and asked me about my thumb. I showed it to her and she said to me that only one treatment could not have possibly cured it. So I told her how I was cured by Brother André and Saint Joseph.

[About the Healings]

(The witness relates many other miraculous cures obtained through the mediation of the Servant of God while still alive.) (Trial, pp. 104-105)[10]

(Trial, pp. 135): I can relate many other healings. Having frequented the Oratory for thirty years, I must have seen hundreds of healings, perhaps even a thousand. Aside from the healings, I can attest to having brought many people to the Oratory and that all, though not all were cured, came back satisfied.

I would like to add the following event. Once, I believe it was in August 1918, many pilgrims had come from the United States. In the morning, seven ambulances had come to the Oratory. By noon, another ambulance had arrived. Brother André was on his way to have lunch. I saw a man talk to Brother André who then went to the ambulance. Near the vehicle, a sick person was lying on a stretcher which had been brought by the ambulance. He was bound to the stretcher. Brother André said, "Release him" and then simply went to lunch. I was surprised to see Brother André leave without looking at the result of his intervention. The person was cured and there was great rejoicing in the surrounding crowd.

---

[10] From the editor's translation of the original Latin version.

Every time Brother André advised someone to not undergo surgery and the surgery took place, the patient would die.

On the other hand, when Brother André told someone to undergo surgery, it would be a success.

Brother André told me that some people were not healed because they did not have the right disposition, that they did not pray enough or that they would not adequately follow the rules of Christian morality.

To others, the religious or the nuns, he would say, "It's worth more to you to suffer."

When people were too insistent about being healed, Brother André would ask them if the Good Lord owed them something. He said that the best way to be healed was to submit to the will of God.

I have already mentioned above the means he employed to heal people. He always recommended submission to the will of God.

When Brother André recounted stories of his cures, he would usually say, "Our Good Lord is so good. These healings are good for those were healed as well as for those who hear about them; it increases their faith." I was under the impression that he healed the bodies in order to get to the souls. He recommended prayer; a persevering prayer.

(Q. 51, *trial,* p. 137): Never did I hear Brother André boast about what happened at the Oratory. He attributed everything to God and to Saint Joseph. He used to say, "Our Good Lord is good indeed! Saint Joseph is so good!" In large public gatherings, he was almost impossible to find, except when obedience called for his presence.

[Brother André Amidst His Occupations]

(Q. 52): I knew Brother André for thirty years and spent entire days in his office, even on hot, suffocating days when pilgrims flocked to him from morning until night. I noticed that he always had a good word for everyone. He was joyful and at the end of the day, he would have the same pleasant disposition that he had at the beginning. So it went, for the first twenty-five years that I knew him. In the last five years as he got older, he would tire more easily and was more irritable. Sometimes, he used harsh words, but it was a way of trying people's faith, of which I have related in an earlier example.

(Q. 53): Sometimes, he seemed sullen, but he explained to me that it irritated him to hear people ask him to perform a miracle or insistently say, "I must be cured."

I ascribe the nervousness of his last years to a lack of energy. After spending long days at the parlour, he was exhausted and sometimes spat blood.

[Brother André and Faith]

(Q. 54): As far as I am concerned, Brother André was a man of unshakeable faith, a faith such as I have never seen. Everything he did spoke of his great faith. He would refer everything back to Our Good Lord. He prayed almost continuously and told me that if people did not get cured it was because they lacked faith.

(Q. 55): When he wanted to build the Oratory, he asked Archbishop Bruchési for the necessary authorization. Archbishop Bruchési asked him if he had had a vision concerning the matter. Brother André replied, "I have great faith in Saint Joseph and it is this that inspires me to do this work."

(Q. 56, *trial,* p. 142): Very often, he asked people if they had faith and in what manner they proved it. He recommended that they follow the commandments of God and of the Church. He told me that someone who has lost his faith has lost God. Once, as I was speaking about a freemason I knew, Brother André told me, "Tell him to pray to God, to put his faith in him."

When he met people who had little or no faith, he would take a crucifix, speak to them about the Passion of Our Lord and endeavour to inspire faith in them.

(Q. 57): He told me that he once met a young lawyer who had lost his faith while he was studying in Paris. He urged him to return to his original faith.

He invited Protestants to pray at the Oratory. I heard that many Protestants and even Jews converted following healings that took place at the Oratory.

[The Children]

(Q. 58, *trial,* p. 143): I have been told that he took advantage of the time during which he cut children's hair to tell them about the goodness of Our Lord and of Saint Joseph. He did the same when he replaced a school monitor during recess.

There were few occasions for him to talk to children at the Oratory. On the occasions that he would see a child, he would give him some good advice, tell him to be a good child, to be obedient.

I never had the good fortune of seeing how Brother André taught the unlearned, except in the situations I have mentioned above, where he taught the sick about the goodness of God and the Passion of Our Lord.

[His Readings]

When he had time to rest, he read the *Imitation of Christ* or about the life of Saint Gertrude or other saints. He would then invite us to join him when we were around, and would provide us with explanations about what he had read.

[His Devotions]

(Q. 59): Brother André had prayers dedicated to the Holy Trinity. When he prayed, either with us or by himself, he often ended his prayers by crossing himself three times and always took care to cross himself perfectly.

When he spoke about the Passion of Our Lord, he started from His childhood up to the sufferings of Our Lord; narrating the whole life of Our Lord. He often said that Our Lord had come to earth to suffer for us.

[Serving at the Altar]

(Q. 60): He loved the liturgy. In the early years, he would serve all the masses said at the Oratory. He avowed that he had often served seven or eight masses in a row. He also helped decorate the altars. To that effect, he kept fresh flowers in his room which he watered and took care of for the sacred services at the Oratory.

In the early years of the Oratory, he would wash the floors of the chapel. He admitted that before many great celebrations, he would get up at night to make sure the chapel was tidy. He took great care of the ornaments as well as the altar cloth. Everything was always impeccable.

When he served mass, he rarely seemed distracted.

Once a server hung a veil on the crucifix. Before removing the veil, he told the child, "A crucifix is not a hanger."

He worked until very late at night to prepare everything in the chapel.

When attending liturgies or masses, he seemed to be in such intimate contact with God, that he projected happiness in all the liturgies of worship.

It is my belief that he did everything he could to make the liturgies more beautiful, more moving.

He attended all the offices he could, and did so with great devotion.

He rang the bells for the Angelus for many years.

In the days of the small chapel, it was Brother André who would clean it. Later, when the crypt was built, he left its care to others.

[Communion]

(Q. 61): It was truly a beautiful sight to observe Brother André come before the holy altar. His expression was different from others'. After communion, when he resumed his place, he would kneel for a long time as if in a state of ecstasy.

Each time I saw him receive Holy Communion, he always impressed me by his posture and pious countenance.

He often visited the Blessed Sacrament where he remained praying for long periods of time.

He would bring us with him to pray in the chapel before he went out to visit the sick. He would pray there for a fairly long time.

When he visited the sick, he would sometimes ask us to bring him to the church where he would pray for an hour or more.

As I have said at a previous hearing, he often went to pray at night before the tabernacle.

In church, I do not think I ever saw Brother André other than on his knees. During the Hours of Adoration, he would remain on his knees, without support of any kind for his elbows, his head bent in prayer.

In his room above the sacristy of the chapel, there was a small window overlooking the chapel. I often saw him pray there and I even prayed there with him myself.

When he prayed, it would be for an hour or more. He was motionless and seemed absorbed in God. When I prayed with him, my legs would go numb. I would have to stand, but he didn't seem to suffer from anything.

(Q. 63, *trial,* p. 148): His manner in church and at communion had in itself the same effect on people as that of a sermon.

He recommended to those who visited him to make novenas and to receive daily communion if possible, according to their confessor's council.

An alcoholic who used a lot of profanity came to see Brother André who then asked the man if he wished to amend his ways. The man answered that he did, so he told him, "Go to communion at least every Sunday."

He would ask [people] if they went to communion often, and helped them understand, by means of comparisons, the necessity of frequent communion: "Should you eat only once a week," he would say, "How could you live? The same goes for your soul. Nourish it with the Holy Eucharist if you want to live."

He spoke to people about matters which were of interest to them, but he always ended the conversation by speaking about Holy Mass and Communion.

One day, a man came to see Brother André who received him in his room as a guest for a few days. I asked Brother André if the man would be cured. Brother André replied, "You know, when you are near God and you don't bother to pray to Him, you cannot expect to be cured." By this he meant that the man did not pray enough to be healed.

I talked to [Brother André] about a man who had asked for my counsel. He said to me, "Tell him to confess often, but as for communion, leave that matter to his spiritual advisor."

A young religious who had become somewhat neglectful of his duties came to see Brother André. Brother André advised him to receive communion regularly and added, "You cannot serve two masters; God and the devil."

[Scripture]

(Q. 64): From my observations, I can say that he seemed to know the Holy Gospels by heart. He would often talk about them, narrating the parables and the Passion of Our Lord according to the Holy Gospels. He advised us to read the Gospels frequently and would explain to me what he had just read.

Brother André would never fail to attend a religious ceremony whenever his duties permitted, whether or not there was a sermon. Later, given the large number of pilgrims, his superiors exempted him from attending a number of religious offices.

Sometimes, I would keep him informed about what had been said at the Sunday afternoon sermon and he was interested by all that I would tell him.

[The Pope, and the Superiors]

(Q. 65): When he talked about the Supreme Pontiff, he would comment on the sufferings of Pius IX[11], on how we were all his children, that among the enemy party in Spain there were also children and that we should pray and suffer for him.

During [Brother André's] last illness, he enquired about the Pope's health, who was then also ill. I have frequently been told that he offered his life for him.

I believe that he loved the Supreme Pontiff, that he revered him enough (he even used to say that he was God on earth) to accept his decisions without doubt.

He obeyed his Superior at the Oratory to such an extent that should he have chosen to disobey someone, he certainly would not have chosen the Pope.

The word of his Superior was a command to him. When he was at my home, gravely ill, his Superior, Father Clément, c.s.c.,

---

[11] *Sic,* or rather Pius XI?

phoned to tell me to make sure that Brother André went to the hospital. I asked him to wait a moment in order to get Brother André's answer. When I told Brother André that Father Clément wished him to be admitted to the hospital, Brother André said, "Tell Father Clément that I am ready to leave at once, if he that is what he wishes."

[The Virgin Mary and the Rosary]

(Q. 66): To what I have previously said about his devotion to the Blessed Virgin, I would like to add a word on the number of rosaries he said daily. When he walked from his office to the Oratory, he always had a rosary in his hand. When we visited sick people, he would say the rosary with us, then alone as we covered sometimes up to fifty miles.

In the evening, when he stayed at the Oratory, he would do an Hour of Adoration, then we would go out into the church square and would day the rosary together.

Sometimes he would say one, two or even three rosaries. He prayed this way until sleep took a hold of him. Sometimes when he went to bed, he would ask me to wake him up an hour later. He would then pray again and say the rosary.

He had healed my thumb on the day of the Immaculate Conception and said to me, "Today is a great day. It's the feast of the Immaculate Conception."

He often told those who visited him to pray to the Blessed Virgin. He never advised the same devotion to his visitors. To some he recommended praying to Saint Joseph, to others to the Sacred Heart and to others yet, the Blessed Virgin.

One of the last prayers he said before he fell into a coma was, "Oh Mary, my Sweet Mother and Mother of my Divine Saviour, pray for me."

During the days he spent with us in Rawdon, he mostly sang the hymn *J'irai la voir un jour*[12].

Once when I asked him if he had slept well, he said, "Yes, but when I don't feel sleepy, I go over some hymns to Saint Joseph or to the Blessed Virgin. I go over some Psalms and eventually, I fall asleep."

He advised people to pray novenas to the Blessed Virgin, especially if he noticed that [the person to which he was speaking] had no particular devotion to her.

Brother André did not like to talk about himself and did not say much on the subject of his personal devotions.

[Saint Joseph]

(Q. 67): I have already spoken about the devotion Brother André had for Saint Joseph. His devotion to Saint Joseph seemed to stem from the fact that Saint Joseph had lived a hidden life and [Brother André] viewed this as the example to follow.

He spent his life spreading the worship of Saint Joseph. He talked about Saint Joseph to the children when he was porter at the college, to the sick who visited him, and to his friends. To them, he spoke about Saint Joseph and invited them to pray to him.

Among my acquaintances, few must have had a devotion to Saint Joseph before they knew Brother André.

[The Holy Angels]

(Q. 68, *trial,* p. 154): He once told me that he prayed to the Holy Angels before mass. He would say, "Oh Holy Angels, penetrate me with God's gaze at the altar, the very same gaze

---

[12] (Tr.'s n.) ("I'll see her soon in heaven") A nineteenth century hymn.

penetrates you in heaven." He recommended that we pray to our guardian angel often.

[The Holy Spirit]

(Q. 69): He had a great devotion to the Holy Spirit. Before he would do the Way of the Cross, for example, he would recite the prayer "Come Holy Spirit."

He once told me that he had found beautiful prayers in the Life of Saint Gertrude which a man had given him.

[His Prayers]

(Q. 70): They consisted of him attending Holy Mass, receiving Communion, attending to the Holy Hour, saying the Rosary and doing the Way of the Cross. He also knew many prayers that I cannot recall. When he visited the sick, he said prayers to Saint Joseph. In his long prayers, he would recite litanies to the Blessed Virgin and to Saint Joseph.

He often said the Rosary of the Seven Sorrows and the Rosary of the Sacred Heart.

During the Holy Hours, he always prayed out loud; so much so that by the end, his voice was barely a murmur and we could then only hear him with some difficulty.

[Brother André and Hope]

(Q. 71): During his stay at my cottage in Rawdon, he talked about Heaven, the marvels of heaven and he sang the Hymns: *J'irai la voir un jour* or *Au ciel, au ciel, au ciel*[13] .

A person said, "One must be such a saint in order to go to Heaven." Brother André replied, "When we do our best. We

---

[13] ("In heaven, in heaven, in heaven.") Mr. Pichette seems to indicate two distinct hymns, but the first excerpt is a verse (see no. 12 above) of an hymn of which the second excerpt is the chorus.

must have faith in God. It would be an insult to Him to believe we won't go to heaven if [we have tried our best][14]."

All his prayers, his observance of the commandments of God and of the Church, everything proves that his life was directed towards heaven.

(*Trial,* p. 158): He once told me, "You know, we are allowed to wish for death when it is for the sole intent of seeing God."

[His Attitude Toward Money and Donations]

(Q. 72): He was not attached to worldly goods. He once told me that he was not allowed to keep money or to spend it because he had taken a vow of poverty.

When people gave him alms, he would not look at the amount. Regardless of the sum, he would thank people equally and put it in his pocket. In the evening, he would put everything in a large black bag, which he kept in his room. When it was full, he brought it to the Oratory's bursar without looking at the amount inside.

He would tell me that we should not be bound to worldly goods, otherwise we could not be bound properly to God.

At the end of his life, it seems that God wanted to deprive him of his best friends and [He] used various circumstances to fulfil that end.

(Q. 73): A woman once gave him a sum of five hundred dollars. It was a certain Mrs. Marceau. I met her daughter shortly after and she said to me, "How strange! Whether you give Brother André five cents or five hundred dollars, it's all the same to him."

All the money he received, except for the mass stipends, went to the construction of the Oratory.

---

[14] (Tr.'s n.) Lit., "if we haven't tried our best."

He used the money at his disposal according to his superior's permission.

[Trials and Confidence in God]

(Q. 74): From the beginning, when he asked Archbishop Bruchési for permission to build a chapel dedicated to Saint Joseph, His Excellency asked Brother André if he had had a vision in relation to this. [Brother André replied], "No. It's my trust in Saint Joseph that inspires me." I believe he put all his confidence in God. He began every cure by saying, "You must desire the holy will of God."

(Q. 75): When he recounted to us the difficulties he had encountered at the beginning, when people called him 'the old fool' and 'the old feeler', he would add, "It was often after such great hardships that the cause of the Oratory would progress most swiftly."

I once heard that an answer given by Father Clément, then director of the Oratory, caused [Brother André] much grief. He had asked for permission [to do something] and Father Clément seemed to make a sign with his hand that Brother André interpreted as meaning he had gone crazy, that he had lost his wits. It caused him much grief because it reminded him of the accusations made against him by his rivals in the beginning. However, he held no grudge against Father Clément, neither did he ever hold one against me, as we had once misunderstood each other, nor against the physician of Côte-des-Neiges who had made complaints about him. In fact, he even later cured his wife, as I have said at a previous hearing.[15]

He never told me whether he had experienced inner difficulties, temptations or any spiritual discouragement.

---

[15] Mr. Pichette's testimony extended over several sessions.

(Q. 76, *trial,* p. 162): I once visited a sick person with Brother André who talked to him about God, His mercy and about the hope of soon going to heaven.

He often told the sick, "Offer your life with a generous heart and you shall not go through the flames of purgatory."

To everyone who went to him, whether seeking temporal or spiritual favours, he recommended submission to the divine will and a great confidence in God.

[Spiritual Direction]

(Q. 77): I believe that there was never anything on his conscience that he did not tell his confessor.

He himself advised others to open their hearts to their confessors.

Father Cousineau, c.s.c., told me that Brother André consulted him mostly about his temptations.

He never meddled with others' consciences. His advice invariably was, "Go see your confessor."

I believe that his confessor knew all about his inner life.

With difficulty and in privacy, he opened his heart to us about troubles. Nevertheless, he hardly ever opened his heart to us. Sometimes we would say, "Poor Brother André, you have endured much, haven't you?" Most of the time, he would make no reply.

He would carefully study the person in front of him before saying anything about himself or his dreams.

[When he confided in others], he never said anything against his fellowman. He was always afraid of disturbing the priests of the Oratory.

[Brother André and the Love of God]

(Q. 78): He would often say, "Our Good Lord is good." His prayers, his Holy Hours and his works of piety are all proof of his love. What seemed to please Brother André the most were the times when he was able to convert a sinner.

In the days of the first chapel, he told a brother of the Holy Cross, "If we could have a priest, we would get many conversions."

When Brother André prayed, his love of God was manifest. After communion, he could spend anywhere from fifteen minutes to a half hour without moving. While he did the Way of the Cross, which could run from an hour to an hour and a half, he appeared to us as if he were filled with the love of God.

(Q. 79): I am inclined to believe that never in his life did he committed a mortal sin. He seemed to love God far too much.

But I do not know.

(Q. 80): I do not know whether he ever deliberately committed venial sins.

(Q. 81): In the difficult times at the beginning, his superiors considered sending him to New Brunswick. When later telling me of this, he said, "I would have been willing to go since it would have been the will of God."

He often repeated to us that one must do the will of God.

(Q. 82): I have already mentioned that I never saw him not in prayer. He told me that when he could not sleep, he went over some hymns and psalms.

During the day, he prayed all the time. Even in the car, during his visits, I would catch him praying and he made us pray. He also liked to chat. In such cases, he would inquire about our business and would talk about the Oratory. Then all of a sudden, he would ask us to say the rosary with him, would speak about religion or summarize a book of piety he had just read.

(Q. 83): In my opinion, he treated everything in his life in relation to God. Everything I have said about his life of piety proves it.

[Facing People's Resistance to God]

(Q. 84, *trial,* p. 166): He once tried to convert a travelling salesman but he did not succeed. He told me about it and expressed his sorrow.

In speaking about communism, he would say to me, "Should they come to get me and chop me up into little pieces, I wouldn't care as long as they would spare the people." And he told me how God was offended by all those societies opposed to the Church. I could also see that such thoughts wore him out.

(Q. 85): One day, I went to a hospital in Montreal with Brother André to see a patient. As we were passing by a room, a patient swore at Brother André, saying that we should not allow people in cassocks in a hospital run by the government. He was swearing and making gestures. Brother André walked over to the patient's bed and asked him, "Are you very ill, my friend? Do you want me to pray for you?" And he added, "I will pray for you." The patient was so surprised by this that he calmed down, lay back in his bed and said nothing more.

Brother André prayed for sinners and he asked people to do the same. When someone ventured to tell a risqué story, he would change the topic. He told me that he used puns to change the topic.

(Q. 86): Usually, when he wanted to convert a great sinner, he spoke about the passion of Our Lord, while holding a crucifix or a statuette of Our Lord covered with blood in his hand. He spoke so well about the love of Our Lord during His Passion, that he hardly ever failed to convert them.

He always spoke about the love of God and it aroused his listeners' love for God.

I can testify that to at least three quarter of the people who came to ask him for temporal or spiritual favours, he would talk of the love of God, tell them how kind He was, urge them to receive communion frequently, to hear Holy Mass, to receive communion well and to pray well.

[His Dedication to His Fellowman]

(Q. 87): He did all he could to help his fellowman. He endeavoured to cure the sick or to soothe them.

He once undertook a long trip to secure employment for my brother-in-law.

He made requests to a company so that my brother-in-law would be able to keep a position he temporarily had to leave due to illness.

He tried many times to reconcile people who hated each other.

He lived in self-effacement. In his room above the chapel, he would lend us his bed while he slept on a miserable mattress on the floor.

He asked people to forgive, to not harbour resentment.

He rubbed people in order to cure them, and sometimes he would do this even after a long and arduous day. Sometimes, he rubbed them for more than an hour. In one case, he did so every night for over three weeks.

He once rubbed me from eleven-thirty in the evening until two-thirty in the morning, without significant rest.

In the first twenty years that I knew him, these rubdowns occurred frequently and lasted for a long time.

He had often said that rubbing oneself is already an act of faith. Did he want to imitate Our Lord who put saliva on the eyes of the blind man? He never told me why he rubbed the afflictions for such a long time. While he rubbed someone, he encouraged that person in an effort to divert the sick person's attention from the pain.

However, I remember cases where the curing occurred without the usual rubbing.

He seemed to love his fellow man, to be obliging in order to bring him closer to God. He always ended a conversation by speaking to people about God and about observing Christian virtues.

(Q. 89, *trial,* p. 170): A young man who had once studied at Notre-Dame College while Brother André was porter, had ceased to practise his religion. One day, he fell sick and was offered a visit by a priest, which he refused. A relative of his went to Brother André and asked him what to do in such a circumstance. Brother André told him to speak to the young man about the little porter of Notre-Dame College, and said "If he wants to see me, I shall go." The young man expressed his wish to see Brother André who advised him to see the priest that the young man had met at the Oratory. The young man gave in to this request, asked for the priest and was converted.

Brother André had spoken to a travelling salesman, whose conduct was bad, about the Passion of Our Lord in such length, that he exhausted himself and started spitting blood. He did not convert the man and told me, "It's sad, he is rejecting grace."

In order to bring souls back to God, he spoke to them about the Passion of Our Lord and advised them to go to confession and communion.

[Corporeal Penance]

(Q. 90): I know that when he was young, his aunt who had raised him, found a chain on his person with which he used to mortify himself. She forbade his using it because he was not strong enough, and he never wore it again.

I never saw him give himself corporeal penance. He never told me if he fasted for sinners.[16]

Once, I saw him eating a dried bread crust with a bit of water. I told him that he shouldn't do that given his state of health. He replied, "What can I say? It would have been wasted otherwise."

[Welcoming and Counsel]

(Q. 91, *trial,* p. 174): I am inclined to believe that all the advice he gave to the sick was to teach them about their faith; as I have stated above.

(Q. 92): He welcomed everyone who came to the Oratory and he listened to them. In certain cases, he advised them to suffer for the Suffering-Christ; as I have heard him tell religious and nuns. He sent people back either cured or at least soothed and encouraged. He sympathised with people who were suffering hardships. Sometimes, he would even shed tears with those who cried.

(Q. 94): Sometimes, I was late for an appointment. He would make me wait for a while by saying a decade of the rosary, then he would greet me.

I have already said that he did not like people insisting on being healed. He was never rude to them, but chided their insistence by asking them whether God owed them something.

---

[16] *To a complementary question (Trial,* Seventh article, p. 250) *the witness later replied*: I heard that when he was young, Brother André subjected himself to mortifications. I have said in my replies to the questions that his aunt caught him wearing a chain, but I must also add that he wore a leather strap with iron points and that his younger cousins told their mother that Alfred often slept on the floor.

To others he would ask, "Do you give orders to your doctor when you consult him?"

I heard him say to some people, "Go to the Oratory, settle the matters of your soul with God and you'll come back with better dispositions."

I have heard that on two or three occasions, he had been somewhat harsh in his replies and he went to see a priest to apologize. The father asked him, "Did you do it on purpose? Did you think about it before?" He replied that he had not, and the priest apparently told him, "Don't worry."

[The Souls in Purgatory]

(Q. 95): He often did the Way of the Cross and usually offered it up for the souls in purgatory.

(Q. 96): He advised us frequently to pray for the souls in purgatory and to do the Way of the Cross for them.

[The Poor]

(Q. 97): He took great care of the poor. He often spoke of the charity we must have for them. He went out of his way to protect the poor.

When I first met Brother André, I was poor and it seems he took better care of me in those days than when I began to earn some money.

He put up some people at the Oratory for charity's sake. It was, of course, with the bursar's permission.

(Q. 98): I think he once told me that we must see God in the poor.

When he learned that we had done good to someone, he promised us rewards from God.

[His Prudence]

(Q. 99): In his work, he always proceeded according to obedience and after having sought proper counsel. He said to me, "We must be cautious in the undertaking of the Oratory. The building's progress is only proportional to the money we receive."

Once, he even approached the architect to show him how cautious we must be in building the Oratory.

(Q. 100, *trial,* p. 177): Once, a young woman complained to Brother André about a priest who was causing trouble in her family. Brother André began to advise her to submit her complaint to the Archbishop, but then corrected himself and told her to see her confessor and follow his advice.

To those who consulted him about their choice concerning a state of life, or how to proceed in certain circumstances, he advised them to pray to the Holy Ghost.

When he counselled people who came to see him to undergo surgery, it was always successful. When he advised them against surgery and they did anyhow, very seldom would they survive it. He never seemed imprudent in those circumstances.

[Modesty and Chastity]

(Q. 101): I once accompanied him to visit his cousin at his home. One day I asked him, "Has it been long since you last saw your cousin?" He replied, "You must have noticed how indecently his wife was dressed, so I don't go anymore."

I mentioned at the last hearing how he would redirect the conversation whenever someone tried to venture [to tell] a risqué story in his presence.

He usually went to the United States twice a year. Except on one occasion, he always wore his cassock, even though the priests themselves wore their clergyman suits.

(Q. 102): In the beginning of the Oratory, Brother André received people mostly during the day. Mrs. Pareau, daughter of a Mrs. Marceau, told me that one day there were many women on their way to pray at the Oratory. In jest she said, "Today, Brother André will be in the company of women." Brother André displayed his displeasure with her and Mrs. Marceau noticed that from that point on, he stopped looking at her and avoided her.

When Brother André received women, he looked down and kept his distance.

He never missed an occasion to tell women that they should dress modestly.

For many years, we kept a stock of coats that we would offer to lend to women who were not properly dressed before they went to see Brother André in his office.

One day, a woman came to Brother André to ask for her daughter's healing. Both the mother and the daughter were dressed immodestly. Brother André asked the mother, "How do you expect to heal her when you are dressed this way, you and your daughter?" And since the mother did not want to promise that she would attire her daughter in a proper manner in the future, he told her it was futile to insist.

I never saw him behave with familiarity towards women. He avoided being alone with a woman except in his office where he received pilgrims. There were, however, windows in his office so that everyone could see what was going on. There always stood a desk between him and the person soliciting a cure.

(Q. 103, *trial,* p. 180): When he had to touch someone, he was very prudent. A man who was afflicted by a hernia asked Brother André to rub him., to which he replied, "Rub yourself, as for me, I fear temptations."

Often, he rubbed over clothes. For the thirty years that I knew him, I never saw him rub a woman.

He advised people to rub themselves by using a medal wrapped in a piece of cloth.

He frequently rubbed me, but always over my clothes or my shirt.

(Q. 104): I received him frequently at my home and he always kept his distance. He was always modest. He was reserved and rather shy.

He never visited a bedridden woman without being accompanied by a family member or the person who brought him to her home. He would ask us to enter the room with him.

(Q. 105): He was usually quite ill when he came to stay at my house. He was always very reserved and saw to it that he would care for himself in more delicate cases. Sometimes, his reserve made us feel uneasy.

I know that he spent some time with a certain Mr. Trudel. I went to see him and sometimes I would take him out to visit sick people. In those days, whenever I went to Mr. Trudel's, Brother André was in a room especially reserved for him.

When he travelled to the United States, he spent nights either in presbyteries or with some friends. There usually was a layman friend who drove him. Sometimes he travelled by train.

He always observed the diocesan rule for travelling by car. He would never sit on the same seat as a woman, and even when the diocesan rule forbade travel by car in the company of women, if there was a woman on board, he would decline the trip.

Moreover, when Brother André travelled by car, he would rarely do anything but pray, by himself or with his companions.

(Q. 106): Whenever he felt he needed to comment on someone's behaviour, whether it was a friend of his or not, he never failed to do so.

[Obedience to God and to the Authorities]

(Q. 107, *trial,* p. 186): He often said that everything must be related back to God; that we must do the will of God. He also said, "Instead of trying to avoid hardships, ask God for the grace to bear them well."

Through all his trials, he submitted himself completely to God.

I never heard Brother André complain about his hardships. He said that it was in times of great trial that his apostolate had succeeded the most.

(Q. 108): As far as I can tell, Brother André submitted to the laws of the Church.

(Q. 109): I never heard him say anything against these laws, and he was so obedient to   his superiors that he must have submitted to the civil laws.

He said we must pray for good government.

[His Courage]

(Q. 110): When he suffered physical pain, he intensified his fervour and piety and would prolong his prayers. At night, he spent two or three hours in bed and worked almost twenty hours. He always suffered from poor health. Someone once asked him, "Brother André, how can you live so long while being of such poor health?" He replied, "By eating as little as possible and working as much as possible."

He was usually cheerful, though he suffered regularly from poor digestion and often spat blood. He spent entire days listening to people's complaints, but used to say that one should not be sad, that it was good to laugh a little.

He suffered from terrible headaches. Often we would find him completely exhausted.

[His Frugalness]

(Q. 111, *trial,* p. 188): I have been told that he usually had a cup of coffee and a piece of bread or a cookie in the morning.

While he stayed at my home during his illness, he ate a hardy meal in the morning and he would hardly eat anything for the rest of the day.

He did not eat much outside the community house. He would have soup, a little meat and rarely had dessert.

He told me once that during the building of the Oratory, he didn't have time to have breakfast before he left the community house. He took three or four small cookies which he put in his pocket, and he forgot about them. He found them in the evening on his way back home. He had not eaten anything the entire day.

I hardly ever saw him eat between meals.

When he was asked what he would like to eat, he used to say, "Anything will do," which made it impossible to know what he liked. When he was served something his stomach couldn't tolerate, he would eat a small amount, which was barely enough, and only in order to please his host.

The priests of Holy Cross often told me that at breakfast time, Brother André would rather spend his time serving the priests who said mass at the Oratory.

We can say that, usually, he barely had one decent meal a day.

Sometimes he cooked for himself. He had an oil stove on which he warmed water and milk and sometimes a kind of stew. He ate standing up while he was working and hurrying in order to be able to leave early to visit the sick.

He only ever drank coffee. I never noticed him eating or drinking excessively; far from it. I remember him once having cognac. He was sick with a double pneumonia. He told me that he was following the doctor's orders.

(Q. 112): At the table, he would have some of whatever was offered.

He never said anything about his tastes. He contented himself with whatever was on the table. He let others serve him and when my wife presented him with the best piece of something, he would refuse it and choose another piece.

Never, to my knowledge, did Brother André eat or drink excessively.

(Q. 113): I do not know exactly. I got to know Brother André when he was 61 years old, and at that time, I was not on familiar enough terms with him to know that.

(Q. 114): He had a good night's sleep once in a while, that is, a few hours. In any case, even the two or three hours of sleep he permitted himself must have been enough for him since he could attend to tiresome occupations for more than eighteen hours or, sometimes, even up to twenty hours the following day.

I believe that he must have gotten the sleep he needed.

[His Participation in Community Life]

(Q. 115): In the first years that I knew him, it seemed to me that he participated quite regularly in the community exercises.

In the last years, when the pilgrims were becoming even more numerous, I know that he attended the early religious offices and that he had breakfast with his community. It occurred to me that his superiors exempted him from other daily religious exercises due to the increasing number of visiting pilgrims.

I do not think he spent his leisure time with the brothers and priests of the community. Later, near the end of his life, he spent that time saying the rosary and his prayers.

My personal opinion on the reason behind him not spending his holidays with the brothers and priests of the community is that he did not want to neglect his self-imposed duties to the sick. During his holidays, he continued his visits to them and to others who solicited his charity.

I can ascertain that Brother André never visited my home without his superior's authorization.

(Q. 116, *trial*, p. 192): One day, having just visited thirteen sick people, he asked me, "Why should we not use modern inventions in order to do good? If I had visited ailing people by tramway or by foot, I could only have seen one or two of them."

He never told me that he liked travelling by car. The people he visited had been recommended to him by people who came to the Oratory and had asked him to visit them.

He never went out for his own pleasure, he rode by car for the sake of seeing the sick.

[His Vow of Poverty]

(Q. 117): He took his vow of poverty seriously. He wore old habits and his overcoat was reddened by constant use as much as by the sun.

One day, as he was coming back from the United States, he stopped by my house. He asked me to count the money he had in his pocket and to keep it, telling me that he could not keep it by virtue of his vow of poverty and that he was quite happy to get rid of it. He asked me to write him a cheque for the same amount, so I did.

I have already said that at the Oratory, he would put the alms he had received from pilgrims in his pockets without counting how much they gave. He would then put the money in a large black bag which he brought to the bursar or to his superior.

Brother André was allowed to give small gifts to those who asked.

Father Clément, his superior, told the woman selling devotional articles that Brother André could give away gifts and souvenirs.

When travelling, he never spent anything. Most of the time, the ticket collectors of the tramway company recognized him and let him in for free. The same was true on toll bridges.

When he was porter at Notre-Dame College, he was allowed to have savings and he probably put that money aside with the bursar. Brother André had too much respect for his vow of poverty, and said to me, "You know, if I died and money was found on me, I couldn't even be buried in the community's cemetery."

(Q. 118): I never witnessed him asking for permission. However, he told me so often that his superiors represented God and must be obeyed in everything, that he must always have asked for their permission.

(Q. 119): I never saw him ask for money from anyone. He gave away souvenirs, rosaries and medals only when he was allowed to, as I have mentioned above.

We gave him a statue of Christ the King, which he later gave back to me. I am sure he had been given permission to do so.

(Q. 120): One day, he came to the shoe store I owned. He showed me his worn-out shoes and asked me whether it would be expensive to have them mended. I made him try on a pair and told him that he could keep them. I threw the old shoes away, but before he left, he asked me for his old shoes back. I told him that they were worn-out, but he replied that it was not for him to decide and that he had to bring them back. So, I gave them back.

I traded his old shoes for new ones on two or three occasions. I used the term 'trade' in order to obtain his consent.

He took care of his clothes. He mended them himself and he made his own pants. When I met Brother André, he wore a light spring overcoat which was already reddened and I saw him wear this overcoat for more than ten years.

He used cedar and naphthalene to protect them from moths and other insects.

In his room, he kept a little cup for personal use. I saw this little cup for eighteen or twenty years.

He was meticulous and very tidy about the way he washed the dishes and the saucepan he used for cooking.

He took great care of the ornaments and the altar cloths when he had the job of looking after them. He even washed the floors of the chapel to make sure everything was tidy.

(Q. 121): Usually, when there was a comfortable chair, he would decline to take it. We had to insist that he use it.

His chamber furniture consisted of a small, narrow bed and a little table. I was told that his bed was made out of wooden boards. He also had two or three little wooden chairs. He was porter at the college at the time.

Later, at the Oratory, he first slept in the little room above the chapel. There were two small iron bedsteads; one could fit two ill men, the other was a single bed. These bedsteads were furnished with a small mattress and a woollen blanket. There was also a small wardrobe where he usually put his pillows and blankets. When both beds were occupied, he would take out from his wardrobe a small mattress and lay it on the floor, and he would sleep on it without a pillow or anything.

Even when he slept in his own bed, he had no sheets and he did not use a pillowcase for his two pillows. He would often sleep over his blanket, sometimes with all of his clothes on. He would only remove his cassock and he seemed used to sleeping this way.

This small room was rather cold. When I slept there, there were some nights when we could have used two or three blankets.

In the later years, there was an oil stove in his room and a cupboard in which he kept spices, some tablecloths and a hand-towel. The chairs, three or four in number, were small and very simple, and they did not have any arms.

There was also a crucifix and two or three wooden framed pictures of Our Lord and a statuette of Saint Joseph.

Later, at the Oratory, his room furniture consisted of a small bed surrounded by a drape (which created an alcove) a small black table without a rug under it, and a wooden armchair without a cushion. There were also two small chairs, a wardrobe for his clothes and a washbasin with running water, the likes of which you would have found in any other room, I believe.

It seems to me that he did not seek personal comfort. This became most obvious when he was offered a comfortable place.

When he came to my home, he was then very ill. He took the bed that he was offered and tried to disturb us as little as possible.

[Additional Information Concerning His Chastity]

(Q. 122, *trial,* p. 199): I have nothing more to add to what I have already said concerning his prudence at interrogations 101, 102, 103 and 104.[17]

When we slept in the room above the chapel, Brother André took his clothes off, or rather went to bed in a darkened room, and a curtain always separated the part of the room he occupied from ours.

At my home, he was excessively prudent and modest.

He would wait for everyone to be in bed and for the lights to be out before he went to the bathroom.

---

[17] Mr. Pichette refers to the question numbers.

(Q. 123): It was extremely rare to see Brother André eating between meals. I answered this question in interrogation 111.

(Q. 124): I have already said that he changed the subject when someone was telling an offensive story in his presence. I never heard him telling an even remotely risqué story himself.

(Q. 125): I answered this question at interrogation 112. Women would say to each other, "With Brother André, we cannot expect special treatment."

(Q. 126, *trial,* p. 203): When I saw Brother André treat an invalid, he would rub the afflicted limb as long as it suited decency. I have, however, never seen him prolong these contacts nor caress the person in any way.

[Mortification]

(Q. 127): After his father's death, he went to live with his uncle. One day, he fell sick and his aunt had to undress him. She found that he was wearing a chain tied by a wire. She told him he was too weak and that he should not wear it. He obeyed her.

He told me that in a part of the college yard, out of everyone's sight, he would bathe in the winter-snow.

He wore a truss because he had a hernia. He admitted to me that he had made it himself. That day, he seemed to suffer a great deal and he admitted that his truss made him suffer. I offered to buy him a truss that would not hurt him, but he declined.

He prayed for long periods of time on his knees, his head bent forward and without any support. He could stay in that position for an hour, an hour and a half or even two hours without moving a limb. It surely was a great act of mortification.

During the penultimate illness of his life, he spent some time at the Hôtel-Dieu Hospital. The nuns told me, "Brother André is going to your home, [we] hope he will eat something other than 'glue'." That is what they called a certain mixture of fine starchy flour and water. They added that he would not eat anything else. When Brother André came to our home, he asked for the same thing and my wife had to ask the doctor to order him to eat what she would offer.

I have seen him eat dry bread and water, rationalizing that the bread was still good and that it would go mouldy otherwise. He would take the medicine his physician prescribed without ever complaining about its bitterness or foul taste.

[Obedience]

(Q. 128): I have already mentioned how he had asked Archbishop Bruchési permission to build a small chapel on the mountain in honour of Saint Joseph.

When his superior went to see Archbishop Bruchési, His Excellency asked, "If we told Brother André to stop receiving the sick, would he obey?" The superior replied that he would do so immediately.

He always obeyed his superiors. He told us so many times that we must see God in our superiors and that obedience could obtain everything [and] that once he was ordered to do something, he obeyed.

I have already given other details about his obedience in previous questions.

(Q. 129): According to my own witness account of events that took place at the Oratory, it seemed to me that Father Laurin, c.s.c., was his spiritual advisor. I drove [Brother André] frequently to Father Laurin's during the time that he was pastor at Saint-Laurent.

In my opinion, [Brother André] did not undertake much without having received advice on the matter from his spiritual advisor.

(Q. 130): I tend to believe that he never did anything contrary to obedience. He spoke too much in favour [of] this virtue. In any case, I never saw him disobey.

[Humility]

(Q. 131): I have already narrated that his superior at Côte-des-Neiges had to answer the door, because there was no porter around. Brother André had asked someone to take his place who, in turn, had left his post himself. The Superior asked Brother André to kiss the ground [to which] obeyed without uttering a word, neither trying to look for an excuse, nor attempting to explain that it was the other brother's fault.

Brother André always seemed to me to be the little dog of the Oratory, just as he had been at Notre-Dame-des-Neiges College.

His humility was evident in all his actions. I never heard him say that he did not share his superior's opinion or that he would have preferred to do something other than what he was told.

I have already mentioned that in the sacred processions and public feasts at the Oratory, Brother André was present only by obedience and in a very discreet manner.

In the chapel of the Oratory, he would remain behind the altar; that was his usual place.

When he was brought somewhere, he would feel uncomfortable if crowds had gathered.

One day, as he was coming back from a trip, Father Clément, his superior, had prepared a welcoming party. Brother André took another path and arrived at the Oratory unnoticed.

His popularity (he was known by everyone) did not move him much.

I have done my share of trips to the Oratory and I can say that, as far as I am concerned, one cannot be humbler than he.

He did not give me the impression that he particularly liked people praising him and he swiftly changed the subject whenever he was praised.

When people congratulated him for his work, his answer invariably was, "Our Good Lord is good indeed! See how Saint Joseph loves us."

Somebody once said to him, "You seem to get a lot of work done around here, Brother André." Brother André answered, "Our Good Lord often makes use of worthless instruments."

[Signs of Impatience?]

(Q. 132, *trial*, p. 208): I never witnessed any fits of impatience towards his fellow religious and I would have been very surprised if it ever happened as he seemed to me to be gentle and patient.

He would be interrupted by the sick during the day, in the evening and at night, but he always welcomed them.

I said at a previous session that he had once been somewhat rude with children but he admitted to a priest, to whom he confessed, that he had done so unwillingly.

I often went to see him at the Oratory, I brought him requests from my family and friends. He rubbed me often and never showed any signs of impatience towards me.

(Q. 133): I never heard him say a word out of vanity or pride. He did not rub with a medal, but with his hand and he repeated this to me many times. He did not believe himself to be more capable than others. It is my belief that he had had a revelation about rubbing without a medal or that he did so because of some kind of inspiration.

[Heroism in the Practice of Virtues]

(Q. 134): In my opinion he practised all the virtues heroically. He was a man of unshakeable faith and absolute confidence in God. In many given circumstances, people of common virtue would have doubted or despaired, while he would be confident that a sick person would get better.

The way he talked about heaven and the joy he displayed that made him radiant were testament to his great hope; the same great hope he would inspire in sinners when he told them about the infinite mercy of God.

In short, all that I have said when answering the questions concerning each of the theological, cardinal and moral virtues lead me to believe that he practised them all heroically. By this I mean that a man of common virtue would not have been able to practise them with such generosity and constancy.

[Supernatural Gifts: Miracles, Knowledge of People...]

(Q. 135): He was blessed with the gift of miracles. One must be either blind or deaf to doubt that.

Out of the two hundred thousand and more signatures requesting the beatification of Brother André, more than eighty percent had obtained favours, graces, healings or miracles from Brother André.

A blind man had come from the United States to meet Brother André. A woman accompanied him. He asked Brother André to heal him and Brother André sent him to pray in the chapel. Usually, when Brother André sent someone to the chapel, he advised them to reconcile themselves with God. That is probably what he told the blind man. Both of them, the blind man and the woman, went to the chapel where they prayed for a long time. I saw them pray and then exit from the chapel. Then they knelt in the old chapel and the woman asked him if he felt any better. The blind man began weeping and I asked him myself the reason for his grief. As he was crying, he explained to me that he had come a very long way and that he was going back unhealed. I went to intercede with Brother André and he received them once more. Then they left. The man was not cured, so I told Brother André: "Your blind man is not cured, Brother André." He asked me whether I knew him. I replied that I did not and I explained how I had met the man. Brother André then said: "It's not well advised to come and ask miracles of Saint Joseph when one comes with someone else's wife." I asked Brother André if the man had confessed this to him. Brother André replied: "There's little chance he would."

To my knowledge, on many occasions, he told people who came to ask him for favours or cures: "Go to the chapel and reconcile yourself with God, then you may come back."

On several occasions, he happened to know things he could only have known by inspiration, for example, when he told people who had come to ask for the healing of someone dear to them: "Go home, the person is cured."

This happened to my cousin, Mrs. St. Germain from Saint Roch, as I have mentioned in question 50. I asked Brother André for her healing. He told me: "As we are speaking, she is feeling better." It was five to three and the very next day, Mrs. St. Germain told me that she had gotten better between a quarter to three and three o'clock.

I have also mentioned that when he was porter at the college, Brother André had inquired with the father of two pupils residing at the college, about his health and that of his family. The man pushed him aside and answered somewhat rudely. A little later, before he left the college, Brother André saw this man again and the latter seemed to regret his harshness. He told Brother André that his wife was home and was ill. Brother André replied that his wife was not ill and that she would answer the door herself upon his return. "Another prophet!" said the man. He went back home and true to Brother André's word, his wife welcomed him at the door. Brother André related this event to me.

One evening, I told Brother André that the wife of Mr. Brosseau, one of my clerks, had gone through surgery on that day, and that she was very ill. Brother André said to me, "She is dead." I told him again that she was merely very ill and he answered me a second time saying: "She is dead." As he told me this, he lowered his head. I looked at the clock and it was twenty to nine.

The next day, the clerk came to the store in tears. He told me that his wife was dead and he recounted how, in the hospital, he had had to monitor his wife in the absence of the nurse. He noticed that his wife did not seem to be breathing and so he called for a nun to see his wife. The nun saw that his wife was dead. At that moment, the clocks in the hospital struck nine. I told Mr. Brosseau that Brother André had announced her death at twenty to nine and I inquired as to whether he had tried to phone Brother André. Mr. Brosseau told me that he had not.

Brother André had often given such answers and we used to say amongst ourselves, his friends, that he could read the past and the future.

A young girl came to see Brother André and asked him for the healing of her sister then gravely ill. Brother André said to her, "Your sister is fine," and when this young girl went back home, her sister had indeed been healed.

Mr. Gadbois, who will come here to testify, went to see Brother André in the middle of the night. His wife had an haemorrhage and the physician had told Mr. Gadbois that it was nearly over for her. Mr. Gadbois went up to the Oratory at three thirty in the morning. He knocked on Brother André's window who said, "Come in, I'll get dressed and we will do the Way of the Cross together. Your wife is fine." True to Brother André's word, after the Way of the Cross, Mr. Gadbois went to his wife and found her completely well. The physician was the most surprised when he phoned the next morning to inquire about the woman and learned that she was cured. And indeed, she was.

I have already recounted the cure of the wife of a physician from Côte-des-Neiges who had been the cause of so much trouble for Brother André and who had come at his wife's request, to ask Brother André that she might be healed. Brother André replied, "I shall go see her, but at this very moment she is well." And it was true.

[Visions and Revelations]

(Q. 136, *trial,* p. 216): The Father Superior of Notre-Dame College was discussing with some people about the future location of the small chapel on the mountain. Father Superior designated a site and said, "The chapel will be erected here. I believe it will be a good location." Brother André immediately said, "It might be better over there." Father Superior replied, "No, it will be here." Brother André quickly answered, "But I have seen it...", but he would not go any further. At that, Father Superior accepted the location that Brother André had pointed out. This event was relayed to me by Mr. Maucotel, who was a witness and who is now deceased.

Father Hupier, c.s.c., was Brother André's confessor. Brother André had asked him which prayer pleased Our Lord the most. Father Hupier recited the Lord's Prayer. He pronounced the words, "Thy will be done" and repeated them three times, and Brother André added, "By that I gathered that I would have to overcome great hardships."

I was told that he had had a vision of the Blessed Virgin with the Infant Jesus. He told her a prayer beginning with, "Oh, my sweet Mother."

One day he asked me, "Do you notice something when we do the Way of the Cross?" I replied that I did not. He told me, "That's strange. I was told that a light appears." Subsequent to this I tried to see it but I never saw anything. I know a man, however, Mr. Fabre, who, as he made the Way of the Cross with

Brother André, had seen a light beaming down on Brother André. He became afraid and immediately left the chapel to tell the priests about it, but they did not believe him at first. He kept repeating this same fact, insisting that he had clearly seen this light. On another occasion, Mr. Fabre saw a light beaming down on Brother André; it was in the evening, while praying before the Blessed Sacrament.

[Manifestations of the Devil]

Question of the office: at the request of the promoter of the faith, the delegated judge asks: Did the servant of God ever witness apparitions of the devil or experience harassment by him?

When the presbytery was being extended, we, Brother and I, went to pray in the crypt. On our way back, we passed through a room where the floor had been removed. At each end there remained a section of a foot or a foot and a half of the original flooring. The depth between the beams and the firm ground must have been two or three feet. The room was about fifteen feet long by ten feet wide. As we were leaning against the wall, Brother André explained to me how the room was to be transformed. He told me how many repairs were required in order to add the new presbytery to the old building, and added, "Our Good Lord is good indeed." But he couldn't complete his sentence. Instead, he took off as though attempting to jump over the gaping hole beside us. He hit his forehead on the piece of flooring at the other end of the room and remained there, his legs hanging, until I rushed over to help. It seemed to me that he had made a twelve foot jump, and I do not know of any man who is capable of jumping such a distance; moreover, Brother André had made a standing jump. He had a lump on his forehead and as he stroked it, the lump vanished. He had also hurt his legs. I was convinced that Brother André wanted to make an imprudent jump, to say the least, but I never brought it up.

The following year, I went to the Oratory and Brother André had lent me the key to his room. I was glancing through a few books while I waited for Brother André. He showed me a book, the life of Sister Marie-Marthe Chambon, and held it open on a particular page. Having returned to his room in the afternoon, I took the book at the designated page and [it read] "I saw that the devil would carry this nun in such a manner[18] and made her suffer." I understood that the leap Brother André had made the preceding year was caused by the devil.

(*trial,* p. 222): He told me that after shrouding the dead, while he was porter at the college, he would usually have a sleepless night. He was alone then, and a black cat would appear to him, making noises which prevented him from sleeping. One night, he heard a row in a room next to his. Fearing that someone had entered into the college, he went to take a look and saw a black cat walking through the glasses in the cupboard. He turned on the light and saw that nothing was broken or displaced.

In the winter [when] I slept in the room above the little chapel, I heard some noise on three or four occasions, as if someone was dragging an iron sheet or chains on the floor of the chapel. One night, the noise was louder and I became afraid. I woke Brother André up and he said to me, "It's nothing. It's nothing." On other nights, when I heard the same noise, I trusted Brother André's words and I did not wake him up.

About four years before he died, Brother André came to my home to recuperate. One night, Brother André rang for me. He told me he felt unwell, that he did not know whether he had had a dream or whether it was real, but the devil had been trying to choke him. I do not think he had been sleeping. He asked me if I had a medal of Saint Joseph and if I could rub him with the medal. I did so. I noticed then that Brother André was sick for he had an irregular heartbeat. Another time, in the little chapel, there occurred a strange event which I have heard many times.

---

[18] (Tr.'s n.) Presumably in the manner described in the preceding paragraph.

A pastor came to see Brother André. Father Clément, c.s.c., told the priest that Brother André was alone in his room above the chapel. The priest went to his room, but as he was nearing the place he was surprised to hear noises, like that of two people fighting and talking to each other. He went back to Father Clément and told him what he had heard. Father Clément replied that he was certain Brother André was alone. The priest went back to the room. He heard the same noises and listened closely at the door. He heard Brother André's voice [saying], "Leave me! Leave me alone! Go away!" Then the priest knocked at the door and entered the room with Father Clément. Upon entering the room, they clearly saw that Brother André was alone.

[Attitude Towards Spiritual Gifts]

(Q. 137, *trial,* p. 225): He never answered us boastfully. He answered using two or three words, in all humility.

When he related events like that of the pupils' father at Notre-Dame-des-Neiges College, I tend to believe that he wanted to strengthen our confidence in Saint Joseph or to tell [us] of the kindness and the might of Saint Joseph. Brother André never boasted about anything. He was very humble, as I have already said.

[Predictions]

(Q. 138): He predicted to my wife the death of my brother, the physician. This was in April, and my brother died in June. My brother was sixty-five years old, but he seemed very well at the time. Brother André was sitting at the table with us and inquired about the health of our relatives. I had to leave the dining room for a moment, and Brother André said to my wife, "One who is about to die is the physician." I overheard the word 'die'. When alone with my wife, I asked if Brother André had talked about one of my sisters who was ill. My wife replied that

74

he talked about my brother, the physician. I was quite surprised and remarked to my wife that my brother seemed to be fine. The following June, on the sixteenth, my brother died suddenly.

I went to see Brother André to ask for the healing of my wife for whom the doctors had given up hope. Brother André replied, "Start a novena, and your wife will start feeling better during the novena." I did so and as a matter of fact, my wife, who had not slept in nine weeks, slept for some time during the very first day of the novena; she was able to sleep for three or four hours without waking. At midnight she woke up complaining that she was tired of sleeping on her side. I helped her change her position and she went back to sleep. She woke up at nine the following morning. She got better as the novena progressed; as I have mentioned at another session.

I visited a certain Mr. Gaudreau with Brother André. Mr. Gaudreau was ill and Brother André said to me, "Your friend, Mr. Gaudreau, will have New Year's dinner in heaven. And in fact, on the first of January, Mr. Gaudreau was dead and his body lay in state in a funeral parlour.

A certain Mrs. Blanchard, for whom I had worked, had talked about hiring me back. I had been hesitant the first time and from that time on she stopped asking me. One day, I related everything to Brother André, asking him whether I should meet Mrs. Blanchard. He replied, "It won't be necessary. Before long, she will come to tell you about it." The very next day, Mrs. Blanchard came to talk to me about hiring me again.

On many occasions he gave such answers to sick people or to us. For instance, to a poor man who was leaving without being cured and who was quite saddened by this, Brother André said, "Go now, and you will be healed on the way." It happened that way.

(*trial*, p. 232): Mr. Dominique Cormier was a conscript in the last war of 1914-1919. My sister, his fiancée, asked Brother André whether he could do anything to prevent her fiancé from being sent to the front. Brother André told her not to worry, that he would not be sent to the front.

Still, Mr. Cormier embarked for England and we later learned that he had been sent to France. My sister told Brother André about it. Brother André replied, "If Mr. Cormier is in France, it's because he requested it. In any case, he won't be sent to the front." Mr. Cormier fell very ill and was sent back home. On his return he told us that he had asked to be sent to France because he was getting bored in England.

In the month of June prior to [Brother André's] death, Brother André stayed at my home for a few days. On three or four different occasions, he told us, "They're going to be incredibly busy at the Oratory."

When he died the following January, I am inclined to believe that Brother André's words were meant to imply the enormous participation of followers that flocked to the Oratory when Brother André lay in state there. It increased the work of the priests of the Oratory because of the numerous confessions they had to hear and the communions they had to distribute.

I can testify that I often heard Brother André give answers predicting what was to happen; subsequently, the events proved him right.

(Q. 139): I have seen nothing of the writings of Brother André. I have never heard that he asked someone to write for him.

[The Last Moments of Brother André's Life]

(Q. 140): If I am not mistaken, I believe that he died from the illness from which suffered throughout his life; a stomach disorder. Later, his arm became paralysed.

(Q. 141): He turned ninety-one on April 9, 1936 and died on January 6, 1937.

(Q. 142): His last illness lasted approximately one week.

(Q. 143): I saw him die, but Brother André had already been in a coma for twenty hours; so I don't know anything significant concerning this question.

(Q. 144): I was told that he had received his Last Rites.

(Q. 149): I know that his last words were, "Oh Mary! My sweet Mother, and Mother of my Saviour, have mercy on me, save me." Then he said a prayer to Saint Joseph. The witnesses heard the name of Saint Joseph, but they did not understand anything else.

(Q. 150): It was on January 6, 1937.

(Q. 151, *trial,* p. 234): He fell gravely ill at the Oratory, but since the Oratory did not have an infirmary, his superiors sent him to Saint-Laurent Hospital some three or four days later.

[His State After His Death]

(Q. 152): I have witnessed many deaths, but when I saw Brother André immediately after his death, I noticed how his face was peaceful looking. I saw him die and was present every day as he lay in state. He was not embalmed. His body was well preserved during those seven days, though it was very warm in the chapel where thousands of the faithful filed past the coffin. I cannot confirm whether the corpse gave off any odour on the last day.

I was at the Oratory when Brother André's body was brought back after the funeral at the Basilica[19]. When they opened the coffin, his head was turned to the right; the

---

[19] Formerly Saint Jacques Cathedral on Dorchester Street, it is now Marie-Reine-du-Monde Cathedral on René-Lévesque Boulevard.

undertaker set it straight and there was no sign of rigidity. It was the fourth day following his death.

[The Funerals]

(Q. 153): The first funeral was held at the Basilica of Montreal on Saturday, January the ninth. The second was held at Saint Joseph's Oratory on Tuesday the twelfth.

(Q. 154): I attended both funerals.

(Q. 155) a) In the chapel of rest.

Brother André's body was carried to the Oratory on the afternoon of January the sixth, and lay in state in the crypt. Many faithful accompanied the body during its transfer. At the Oratory, he first lay in state until Saturday morning—at which time a funeral was held at the Cathedral—then until the following Tuesday, the day of the funeral at the Oratory.

When the body was brought to the Oratory, Father Cousineau, c.s.c., said a few words to the assembly, and from everywhere wailing and sobbing could be distinctly heard.

From then on, there was an uninterrupted flow of the faithful coming day and night from everywhere, even from the United States, either by train or by plane, to pay homage to Brother André's remains.

The faithful brought sick people on stretchers, while invalids suffering from various afflictions came to pray to Brother André, asking for a miracle.

The priests told me that on the occasion of this gathering, there were many extraordinary conversions.

There were confessions throughout this gathering. There were, I believe, eight confessionals and the priests had to add two more in order to satisfy the demand.

Some people spent the last night in the crypt, hoping to get a seat for the funeral. To satisfy these people, the coffin containing the remains of Brother André had to be brought about and shown to the crowd.

Those who filed past Brother André's body often tried to obtain relics of Brother André. They would deposit small pieces of paper on which they had written their intentions, in the coffin or on trays, and would touch Brother André's body with their rosaries and medals.

b) The Day of the Funeral

The funeral at the Basilica was held on a rainy, windy day. The roads were icy and a fine hail was falling. Despite the weather, a large crowd walked the three miles that separated the Oratory from the Basilica.

As for the funeral held at the Oratory, I have said that an estimated crowd of ten thousand people could not get into the already overcrowded crypt.

(Q. 156): People rushed to enter the Oratory and a string of policemen was required to control the crowd.

The news we heard on the radio about Brother André's illness, his death and the great crowds rushing to the chapel of rest came from the news agencies. They had not been solicited by the priests of the Oratory.

No pressure, therefore, was made on the faithful to come pay homage to Brother André.

(Q. 157): The visitors who came to the chapel of rest and to the funerals came to pray.

They all wanted to kneel and pray in front of the coffin but were not allowed to do so due to the size of the crowd. They touched the feet of Brother André with their rosaries and medals.

When they had passed before the coffin, most of the people knelt in the crypt and prayed.

At long intervals a rosary was said, to which the crowd responded.

(Q. 158): The body of the Servant of God was interred in a small room next to the crypt of the Oratory. It was not closed from the crypt in order to allow the faithful to come to pray. The coffin was sealed in the afternoon following the last funeral.

The night Brother André passed away, Dr. Lamy removed his heart and the Holy Cross priests put it in a sealed glass jar, now kept in the office Brother André had used when he was alive. Many people still pray before Brother André's heart.

(Q. 159): It has not been moved. The coffin is kept in a recess in the crypt which was built especially for it, and the expenses were covered by the premier of the province of Quebec at the time, the Honourable Mr. Duplessis[20].

He is therefore not truly in the crypt but we have access to his tomb by the crypt. There is a Latin inscription saying "Here lies Brother André, poor and humble"; well, that is the gist of the inscription.

[The Veneration of the Faithful]

(Q. 160): The testimonies of veneration are spontaneous. Very rare are those who come to pray to Saint Joseph at the Oratory without going to pray at Brother André's tomb[21].

One day, as we were maybe forty of fifty people praying at Brother André's tomb (it was a time of individual prayer for each of us) His Excellency Gauthier, Archbishop of Montreal,

---

[20] Mr. Maurice Duplessis had been a student at Notre-Dame College, where he had gotten to know Brother André.

[21] The drawback is that no one can be proposed for public veneration until Rome authorizes the cult.

came at that very moment and said, "Well, that's it! Pray to Brother André! Ask him for favours."

(Q. 161): I never saw any form of planned testimonies of veneration at Brother André's tomb. There had been, for some time, public prayers asking for his canonization, but it has ceased long ago.

(Q. 162): On August 9, 1940, at around eleven in the evening, a nine year old boy came to ask to for a healing. The child had never been able to walk without a pair of special boots with an iron brace going up to his knees. His boots were taken off and put near Brother André's tomb. The young boy, sitting on the bench, jumped indicating to everyone that something extraordinary had happened. Brother Pierre, c.s.c., took the little boy in his arms and put him on Brother André's tomb. When the little boy told Brother Pierre that he felt no pain, the brother let him walk and he walked to the altar in his socks. He was cured.

I have heard that there were many cures and miraculous happenings at Brother André's tomb, but I have not witnessed any.

(Q. 163): No, the relics of Brother André are not publicly venerated.

(Q. 164): One can say that there is always someone present at Brother André's tomb. Practically no one ever goes to pray in the crypt without praying at the tomb.

On Sundays, feast days, or novena days it is usually necessary to have people direct the pilgrims in order to give everybody a chance to get to the tomb.

I have seen for myself representatives from all classes of society. If there are more poor people, it is because this class is most numerous.

(Q. 165): The number of pilgrims at Saint Joseph's Oratory seems to be increasing, and I have said above that those who come to pray at the Oratory usually go to Brother André's tomb.

The number of devotional exercises has been increased and consequently the crowds at the Oratory are more numerous.

(Q. 166, *trial,* p. 243): The priests do not need to resort to human industry[22] as the crypt's chapel is always filled with the faithful.

[Reputation for Saintliness]

(Q. 167): I do not believe that there are many people who have met Brother André and do not believe that he was a saint.

All were convinced that Brother André obtained from God whatever he wanted. Those who saw miracles obtained by the intercession of Brother André could draw only one conclusion: he was indeed a saint.

I heard some time ago, that over two thousand people signed a petition requesting the beatification of Brother André.

Brother André was universally known. People came from everywhere in Canada and the United States to ask for a healing, a temporal or a spiritual favour.

[Cures After the Death of Brother André]

(Q. 169): I mentioned the other day the healing of the young boy, in *Question 162*.

A certain Mrs. Grenier from Rawdon was afflicted by angina. She had asked for a relic of Brother André. A year later, I saw the woman. She told me that after wearing the relic of Brother André, she never had a fit of angina again.

---

[22] That is human means, such as advertising for example.

I have read, in the *Annals of Saint Joseph's Shrine*, many accounts of extraordinary favours obtained by the intercession of Brother André after his death. For instance, a nun whose knees made her suffer was suddenly cured during the night of the seventh and the eighth of January 1937, that is, two days after Brother André passed away.

I have witnessed many events in which, by the intercession of Brother André, people obtained temporal favours. Some such examples are the paying off of debts that were considered a complete loss and the healing of certain illnesses.

The *Annals of Saint Joseph's Shrine* often announce a person's healing by the intercession of Brother André and others obtained by the intercession of Brother André and Saint Joseph.

A sister of mine who had been ill all her life was in such a state last year that Dr. Dumas, who was treating her, told me in November 1940: "This woman should have been dead since October." She had never weighed more than seventy-five pounds. Her body had swollen all over, to the extent that she could not walk anymore. She made novenas to Brother André and she got better. Though she did not get completely better, her state of health had greatly improved nonetheless.

Before his death, Brother André had promised that the priests would never lack the funds for the completion of the Oratory. For some time, little money boxes have been placed in homes to collect donations for the Oratory. The money flows to the Oratory and the people who send this money usually add a little note. It invariably says, 'for a favour received', for such events as in thanksgiving for a healing or for finding a job, for instance.

[Heroism in the Practice of Virtues]

(Q. 170): I have often had the experience of seeing Brother André in my dreams, giving me advice, telling me what I should do. It seems quite extraordinary to me.

I would like to add that in the practice of virtues, of all the virtues, all that Brother André did and all that he thought was boundless and practised in complete disregard for himself. The daily repetition of all his acts of charity towards his neighbour, the way he received visitors throughout the day, his hearing nothing but complaints and the long evening prayers at the Oratory, all show his heroism in the practice of charity. Brother André sometimes called on young priests to pray with him at the Oratory. The priests found it so tiresome and difficult that they hid on the following days in order to not go with him.

In my opinion, he practised all the virtues to the highest degree. I have shown that his charity was extraordinary, as was his piety and his virtue of faith. It is my belief that a man who practises these virtues in this way must practise all virtues in the same way, since they are all linked one to another.

(Q. 171): I have nothing further to say. **[End of testimony]**

To obtain a Favor through Blessed Brother André

O God, You who are most admirable in Your saints, we petition You to grant us through the intercession of Blessed Brother André, the apostle of Saint Joseph, the favor which we ask: [..], so that we may be led to imitate his virtues. Through Jesus Christ, Our Lord. Amen.

For the Canonization of Blessed Brother André

O Jesus, you who wanted the devotion to your foster-father Saint Joseph to be made known through the efforts of Blessed Brother André, grant that the Church may glorify, at the earliest opportunity, your faithful friend of the poor, the sick and the afflicted. Saint Joseph of Mount Royal, pray for us. Amen.

Calvary offered by J. O. Pichette and his wife (see page 3)

Contents

LUMIÈRE SUR LA MONTAGNE

1- Roland GAUTHIER, c.s.c., *Brèves réflexions sur le patronage de saint Joseph*, 22 p.

2- Marcel MONGEAU, o.m.i., *Saint Joseph, époux bien accordé à Marie*, 62 p.

3- Roland GAUTHIER, c.s.c., *La dévotion à la Sainte Famille en Nouvelle-France au XVIIe siècle*, 74 p.

4- Michael D. GRIFFIN, o.c.d., *Saint Joseph. A Theological Introduction*, 52 p.

5- René LAURENTIN & André DOZE, *Présence de saint Joseph chez Bernadette Soubirous*, 36 p.

6- Pierre ROBERT, *Saint Joseph dans l'unique Seigneur. Sur les fondements spirituels d'une dévotion*, 22 p.

7- Paul-Émile LÉGER, *Le Cardinal Léger et l'Oratoire Saint-Joseph. Textes choisis*, 42 p.

8- Joseph F. CHORPENNING, o.s.f.s., *The Holy Family Devotion. A Brief History*, 74 p.

9- Roland GAUTHIER, c.s.c., *Saint Joseph dans l'histoire du salut. Exposé biblique et théologique*, 26 p.

10- René LAURENTIN & André DOZE, *Presence of Saint Joseph in the Life of Bernadette of Lourdes*, 38 p.

11- José de Jésus Maria, o.c.d., *Présence de Saint Joseph chez Thérèse de Lisieux*, 34 p.

To order:

Research and Documentation Center, Saint Joseph's Oratory
3800 Queen Mary Road
Montreal (Quebec) Canada, H3V 1H6
Phone 514/733-8211, ext 2331. E-mail: crdosj@iquebec.com

www.saint-joseph.org